THE SECRET PLACES

ANN AND MYRON SUTTON
Photographs by the Authors

RAND McNALLY & COMPANY
CHICAGO · NEW YORK · SAN FRANCISCO

THE SECRET PLACES

WONDERS OF SCENIC AMERICA

Other Books by the Authors

Stellar of the North
Nature on the Rampage
Exploring with the Bartrams
Guarding the Treasured Lands
Journey into Ice
Animals on the Move
The Life of the Desert
Among the Maya Ruins
The Appalachian Trail
The American West: A Natural History
New Worlds for Wildlife
The Wilderness World
of the Grand Canyon

The photograph on page 1 was taken along the Inside Passage, Alaska; pages 2 and 3, view from Sandy Cove, Glacier Bay, Alaska; page 13, Johns Hopkins Inlet and Glacier, Glacier Bay; page 15, Lava Beds National Monument, California; page 117, Little Buffalo River Valley, Tennessee; page 159, Martin Lake, near Kennebec River, Maine.

The Hawaii Natural History Association has kindly given permission for the photographs of the restored temple of Hale-o-Keawe, City of Refuge National Historical Park, shown at top, pages 62 and 63.

Book Design by Mario Pagliai

❧ CONTENTS

Introduction 🌿

SHE GOT OUT OF HER CAR AND WALKED BRISKLY INTO THE ranger station. There was a look of determination in her eyes. People did not usually look that way when they came back from Montezuma Well. More often they stopped to let the ranger know what a good time they had had. Now a tempest seemed imminent.

"Ranger!" she commanded, as if to summon the National Park Service, the Arizona Highway Patrol, and the gods of Olympus.

"What did you think of the Well?" the ranger asked, smiling.

She put her hand on her hip in an impatient way, and he knew that she was not going to answer his question.

"Why are you keeping this place secret?" she asked.

There was a moment of silence. The ranger shrugged his shoulders with a knowing air. He was about to answer when she spoke again, repeating.

"Why are you keeping this place secret? We never heard of it. It's just a little green square on the map. A person could see those signs on the road and go right on by."

She paused for a moment, and he knew she was only groping for words.

"Why don't you advertise?"

"Well," he said, "we just don't have an advertising budget."

"You ought to."

"Our first task is to preserve and protect these areas and the people who visit them. We give information and help the best we can and that is a full-time—"

She turned her head away. "It's a shame! It irritates me when I think how we almost missed something terrific. What about other people? Everybody in the country ought to see this place and you're keeping it secret."

He smiled again. "I take it you had a good time."

"Did we! We almost never got away. The kids went down inside. My husband snapped pictures of the Indian ruins along the rim. And when we got to the spring—what a cool and beautiful place on a hot day! I could have sat there for hours . . . ."

*   *   *

This story is not only true, but also a common occurrence. We experienced it, or some version of it, frequently at remote outposts of the West and East. The dialogue is familiar and almost invariably consists of three central themes: you are keeping this place secret; you ought to advertise; and everyone ought to see it.

Montezuma Well, of course, is not secret and never has been. In fact, none of the areas in this book is actually secret. None is hidden. They are available to all persons who wish to visit them, all who can find them, all who can perceive what is in them.

Some are hard to reach. Some require considerable hiking. Some hold discoveries that take a good deal of persistence to make. Mostly, though, they require a certain quality of perception on the part of the human observer.

And that, perhaps, is a key to the reason for this book. When we hear men deplore the human condition, the collapsing environment, war, wages, pestilence, the future, or simply the way things are, we hope they are not forgetting that just a few miles away, or next door, or beyond the horizon is a milieu of wonder and beauty where things are still as they used to be, or almost so.

New York has its Bear Mountain; Chicago, its forest preserves; Los Angeles, its national forests; New Orleans, its bayous; Miami, its Everglades.

Close by lies a world where our jaded souls can be refreshed as fully as a tree is washed by rain. Somewhere, readily reachable, is a place or a string of places that have been saved and preserved by the foresight of our ancestors for the very reasons we need them now: to be alone, to explore, to discover, to revel in the sheer joy of living. This is what we want to share in our book, because we have found such places, hundreds of them, and have been infinitely inspired.

The "secret places" are secret only if we never hunt for them, or never find them for ourselves.

Of course, the city environment must be improved, and we must protect our marshes and shores, and we have to keep alert in daily chores and daily jobs. These are times of hard work. But man can laugh, he can hope, he can love, and lest these singular attributes atrophy, he must take himself away, now and then, from whatever disturbs him.

The principle is not universally accepted, but we believe that a man who likes to dream or to think or to place himself in perspective needs to go where a coyote calls, or a gull floats over the sea, or where, as Thoreau said, he may in some historic place become separated from himself.

There are secret places all over this country, this continent, and this world where man can do these things, and where he can explode, let off steam, dance, sing, shout, relax—where he can do things differently and become separated from all but his soul.

This book tells of ten outstanding places we have discovered where just such things can be done with pleasure. You will not, perhaps, seek similar surprises or be thrilled by the same adventures, for these voyages to our secret places are personal ones. But there is something for everyone, an obvious reward in the search for one's own secret worlds. There is always too much to see. We never have enough time. Discoveries pile on discoveries.

We prepare in advance. We study. We check the maps. We go. On arrival we slow down and unwind. We stop and listen. We learn. We enjoy. And in the end we surrender to the wind and the music and the fragrance, and there is to us no other energizing influence quite as strong.

To enjoy the quiet and solitude, to feel the thrill of discovery, to see unfolded the pages of the past in historic sites, in a way represents a frontier of the human mind. It is a frontier that needs a seeing eye. The "secret places" are open secrets, but they must be discovered and rediscovered if they are to renew our energy and freshen our thoughts.

We can be blind; we can be poor; we can be crippled—but there is a universe in every leaf, and love in every flower. We have no intention of being abstract or obtuse about this; you will discover in the first chapter that Glacier Bay, Alaska, demonstrates the very pulsations of our enormous universe.

There are places where we discover, not once but often, that a wanderlust within us waits for kindling sparks, and that we ourselves ignite it if we open our hearts to the worlds from which our daily existence may have insulated us.

Thousands of secret places are available; we need only seek the nearest as an antidote to a world that sometimes moves too rapidly for the human system.

The criteria for our selection of these ten particular secret places—and we had to select arbitrarily somewhere—were: one, that each be not well known, not like Niagara Falls or Bellingrath Gardens or the Grand Canyon; two, that there be examples from each geographical region, encompassing all kinds of scenery; three, that there be a link to the national heritage and a meaning of some sort for all human beings of the country and the world; four, that the site possess something of interest in several major fields, such as science, history, and archaeology; five, that there be ways to enjoy the places and plenty to do—trails for hiking, water for swimming, tours, meaningful exploration; and six, that each place be so complex that many discoveries could be made, with many obviously waiting to be made when we left—no matter how many times we might return, the old miracles would be renewed and new ones revealed.

When we visited each area we sought the help of persons highly competent in the fields involved, persons who knew where we ought to look, who knew the natural or historical or archaeological background, and who could give us different philosophies. We often recorded personal interviews on tape. Some persons made long lists of information sources for us. Some took us on patrol trips or extended flights or rock-climbing expeditions. Some hiked with us and opened our eyes to unexpected treasures along the way. All took valuable time from important schedules, and we are more grateful to them than we can say. They cannot be responsible for what we write, though many reviewed the manuscript and picked up errors or misinterpretations.

It is impossible to name everyone who provided the help, advice, and good counsel that went into the making of this book. We thank them all, and particularly the following:

General: Michael and Larry Sutton tramped many a trail with us in gathering data and illustrations, and without them the book could never have been as complete as it is; their professional skill in handling tape recorders, cameras, notebooks, research materials, and camp equipment places us in their debt forever. We are also deeply obliged, for help on more than one chapter, to Agnes M. Allen, Mr. and Mrs. George Baggley, Edward P. Cliff, John E. Doerr, Mr. and Mrs. Frank F. Kowski, Jennie M. Livesay, Charles Marshall, John Rutter, Lola F. Smith, Mr. and Mrs. John Stratton, Goldie Marie Sutton, Len Volz, and Mr. and Mrs. Herman L. Womack.

Glacier Bay: June Branner, Mr. and Mrs. Robert Howe, Mr. and Mrs. Charles Janda, and Greg Streveler.

Lava Beds: Mr. and Mrs. William J. Kennedy, Jerry Lee, and Harry Sprouill.

Place of Refuge: Russell Apple, Gene J. Balaz, Al Carrillo, Dwight Hamilton, T. Hewitt, Fred Johnston, and E. Ladd.

Verde Valley: Harold S. Colton, Mr. and Mrs. John O. Cook, Harvey Koller, John F. Lance, Allan Phillips, Mr. and Mrs. Lloyd Pierson, Mr. and Mrs. Douglas Rigby, and Mr. and Mrs. Paul F. Spangle.

Arches: J. F. Carithers and Mr. and Mrs. Bates Wilson.

Prairie du Chien: Walter Barrett, Paul F. Beaubien, Florence Bittner, Robert T. Bray, Jacquelyn Lamb, Wilfred Logan, Gary Matlock, Gordon Peckham, Robert K. Searles, and Milton Thompson.

Natchez Trace: Garth Adams, Guy Braden, Gil Calhoun, Charlotte Capers, Mr. and Mrs. James E. Estes, Roger Giddings, Mr. and Mrs. Jacob Hamilton, Robert C. Haraden, Keith Miller, Ken Morgan, Tom Pardee, Don Pumphrey, Guy Taylor, Richard L. Vance, and the ladies of Rosalie Mansion in Old Natchez.

El Yunque: Ricardo Alegría, Miguel Barasorda, R. P. Briggs, Máximo J. Cerame-Vívas, Ricardo Cotte, Carlos Diago, Enrique García Díaz, His Excellency Governor Luis A. Ferré, Gabriel Ferrer, María E. Figueroa, Luis M. Juarbe, Henry Klumb, Sr. y Sra. Julio Marrero-Nuñez, Mr. and Mrs. James Metcalf, Manuel A.

Morales, Carlos Muñoz, Rosa Navarro de Haydon, Victor Olazabal, Eduardo Ortiz, Rafael Picó, Carlos E. Ramírez, Otto Octavio Reyes, Pedro Salazar, J. Charles Tracy, Frank Vilella, Frank Wadsworth, and Robert Wize.

Quantico Creek: Nash Castro, W. Drew Chick, C. Kenny Dale, Amos Hawkins, Theodore T. Smith, and Maurice Sullivan.

Ann and Myron Sutton

THE
SECRET
PLACES

The WEST

🌿 The WEST

So MUCH SCENERY LIES STRETCHED OUT WIDE, OR UP AND down, in western North America, and so many canyons, gullies, coves, beaches, peaks, and forested vales exist that selecting certain secret places as representative seems more than a trifle presumptuous. Almost everyone, seemingly, knows of the famous localities; to choose among lesser wonders is only to make some personal decisions based on private experiences.

But that is the obvious part of it. Each man's list of secret places, different from others to be sure, is his own proud, personal possession. For the West we have singled out localities in Alaska, California, Hawaii, Arizona, and Utah, partly because these are a few of the ones we know best.

Yet a chapter could be written on Liard Hot Springs in Yukon Territory, where a luxuriant forest and wild flower gardens surround a series of steaming, bubbling, prismatic springs just off the Alaska Highway.

The story of the landslide at Frank, Alberta, has been often told, but few people know of it. British Columbia is full of history, and as for pristine, primitive beauty (the offshore islands, the Fraser River), it can rank with Alaska at the top of the list.

18

In Alaska there is so much pure and elegant territory—wasteland some would call it—that men have had the irresistible urge to pasture exotic reindeer over it, parcel it out to bidders, puncture it with holes, run roads and pipes across it, and otherwise eliminate the one advantage that makes it a priceless treasure today: wildness.

Of this, a great deal still exists, and most is certainly secret to the bulk of humanity. One visit to the Susitna Valley, or the Wood River-Tikchik region, or almost anywhere on the Arctic Slope seems to stir in the souls of men a resolute defense against Alaska's public enemies—such as oil. Men seem to remember most the solitude, the voice of the wolf on faraway tundra, the grizzly mother with her cubs, the yellow green of the sphagnum moss, the flowers . . . .

In Washington State the true significance of Grand Coulee gorge is missed by nearly everyone simply because it is so overwhelming and so obvious; its story of natural rampage is bolder than anything modern man has ever seen. On the other hand there are hidden bogs on the Oregon coast that hold the Darlingtonia, or pitcher plant, an insect-trapping species with delicate color and fascinating botanical characteristics.

You can find in the northwestern rain forests a thousand artistic designs to please the most discriminating taste—the forms of ferns, for example, or the silver glitter of raindrops strung on a hemlock branch, or the silent sifting of mist through veils of vegetation.

In the desert, too, it is often the simple things that matter. The needle pattern on a saguaro cactus trunk was not necessarily meant to please the sensibilities of men, but that it does. A lone leaf left on an ocotillo in autumn summarizes the cycle of life itself. And when, in the early hours of dawn, we hear from a distant draw a pack of coyotes in chanting concert, the music becomes a part of our secret love for a little-known corner of creation.

Perhaps, then, the secret places are essentially indefinable in familiar terms, for it is what we feel that counts.

Glacier Bay, Alaska 🌿

IMAGINE A GALLERY OF GLACIERS AS WIDE AS THE HORIZON and as high as the sky. Sketch into this mental picture an avenue of emerald water leading to the bases of towering peaks. Brush in a bank of mist and add a flock of phalaropes, then place a few hundred seals on blue icebergs.

Pick out the brightest blue sky you have seen. Touch up the picture with kittiwakes flying in circles and grizzly bears walking on the shore. Enter a breath of warm air and tune in the roar of ice cracking, crashing, and booming as though in a celestial chamber of echoes.

You have started to paint an Alaskan version of paradise. It is a distant paradise. No roads lead to it. The symphonies it presents are not heard by humans in formal attire. The sculptures on exhibit in its natural galleries are changed repeatedly, but few persons ever see them.

The great complex of water, ice, air, and life that we call Glacier Bay, vast and virtually unspoiled, lies hidden only because it is located in a land immense enough to hide it. The Yukon Territory, British Columbia, and Alaska all unite here in some of the most spectacular scenery in North America, much of it covered with snow and ice, the final products of incoming tons of moisture from the sea.

20

We came by ship to Juneau, then changed to an amphibious aircraft that flew by way of the Tlingit Indian village of Hoonah to the landing dock at Bartlett Cove, inside the mouth of Glacier Bay, a hundred miles west of Juneau.

Next morning we were out on the water, heading west and finally north into the wide wilderness of water and mountains that is Glacier Bay.

The sea was calm, the swell gentle. Tufts of clouds clung to the sides of mountains and a low, overcast sky still obscured the distant mountains observed the night before.

Almost immediately the action began. Any thought of sitting back and relaxing until we got to where we were going vanished. We were there already.

A massive gray "island" rose slowly out of the water and eased back in, leaving hardly a trace of wake. Humpback whales were out, escorting the boat. With luck, we would see them leap clear of the water.

Abruptly we discovered a world not silent, dull, forbidding, as one might imagine it. Glacier Bay is more than a bay of glaciers. It is a land and sea exuberant with life.

Hundreds of birds flew across the water as we made our way north. Most were murrelets, diving or skittering away as we approached. The murrelet seems about as adapted to flight as an iceberg; the wings appear too small to lift such a chunky load. They beat furiously. The bird flutters across the water, becomes airborne for a moment, plunges back to the surface, skids along and bounces up two or three times before finally getting aloft.

The water surface and the air above it seemed to vibrate with such movements. At times, we were told, hundreds of thousands of northern phalaropes covered the water.

Suddenly we saw an opening in the clouds far in the distance where the sun came through the overcast and shone on a patch of snow at the edge of an inlet. The effect was one of some great mass of candles being lighted, and the glow permeated the bay and the clouds in all directions.

Closer by, a spotlight of sunshine played in slow-motion patterns over the water, its form either circular or elongated, softened or brightened in obedience to the restless clouds.

The mists thinned out and tips of mountains appeared above them. Wisps of clouds skirled over the sides of the peaks, chasing each other around the ridge tops, here or there revealing a rocky slope or a patch of grass and then hiding them again. One string of clouds lay linked like a necklace around a mountain. Transient mists descended into valleys and ravines, or engulfed the forest to the very edge of the sea.

Out on the bay more action occurred than our eyes could follow. Gulls delighted in following the wake of the boat, expectantly searching for bits of food turned up. Birds literally streamed in all directions, toward us, away from us, across our path, fore, aft, and parallel.

Near Willoughby Island the icebergs began to show. At first they appeared as shimmering bits of white on the horizon, but slowly the pieces came together, as in a mirage. Now blue, now green, now white, they assembled into freeform shapes that were both unusual and amusing.

We paused in Johnson Cove. The tide was out, and the glistening rocky shore reminded us that this region possessed a considerable community of intertidal life: rockweed, crabs, clams, limpets, barnacles, urchins, starfish, snails, and mussels. Add the pelagic life farther from shore, and the bay becomes a nursery of rich abundance. No wonder so many birds live here.

Cottonwood trees lifted their arms above the shrubbery ashore. Tufts of "cotton" hung conspicuously among the leaves, and from a distance resembled white flower clusters.

An old abandoned cabin, disintegrating and collapsing at the edge of the woods, gave witness to the many attempts of man to settle in this wilderness, to make something commercial of it, to gain some kind of a fortune where others dared only to survive. But it was no use. Fox farming, for example, failed because the rate of animal reproduction was too low to be commercially profitable.

Moving on, we got a feeling of both the intimate and the familiar, the simple and the complex, the minute and the boundless. Shoulders of high, ponderous ridges nudged through the clouds, and we had for a moment an almost mysterious, chilling feeling of something hidden beyond, something able to swallow us up: as one cannot see where he goes he does not know what dangers, if any, he faces.

This is the thrill of entering the unknown. In such moments we get a sense of what the early explorers must have felt on reaching the unfamiliar regions of the Arctic.

Glacier Bay was almost totally filled with ice when the expedition of Capt. George Vancouver sailed through Icy Strait in 1794. Had he and his men known that a tremendous bay lay off the bow they could have done nothing more than examine the high front wall of the enormous glacier that filled it.

Indeed, Glacier Bay and all its inlets were known only vaguely, through Indian legends, until John Muir, himself almost a legend now and one of the continent's greatest conservationists, arrived in 1879. Accompanied by Indians, Muir had searched a long time to find the bay with great ice mountains about which they talked. Finally, on October 25:

> We got under way about 10 A.M. The wind was in our favor, but a cold rain pelted us, and we could see but little of the dreary, treeless wilderness which we had now fairly entered. The bitter blast, however, gave us good speed; our bedraggled canoe rose and fell on the waves as solemnly as a big ship. . . . About noon we discovered the first of the great glaciers, the one I afterward named for James Geikie, the noted Scotch geologist. Its lofty blue cliffs, looming through the draggled skirts of the clouds, gave a tremendous impression of savage power, while the roar of the newborn icebergs thickened and emphasized the general roar of the storm.

The following day was Sunday, and Muir went out alone,

> . . . pushing on through rain and mud and sludgy snow, crossing many brown, boulder-choked torrents, wading, jumping, and wallowing in snow up to my shoulders. . . . I reached a height of fifteen hundred feet, on the ridge that bounds the second of the great glaciers. All the landscape was smothered in clouds and I began to fear that as far as wide views were concerned I had climbed in vain. But at length the clouds lifted a little, and beneath their gray fringes I saw

the berg-filled expanse of the bay, and the feet of the mountains that stand about it, and the imposing fronts of five huge glaciers, the nearest being immediately beneath me. This was my first general view of Glacier Bay, a solitude of ice and snow and newborn rocks, dim, dreary, mysterious. I held the ground I had so dearly won for an hour or two, sheltering myself from the blast as best I could, while with benumbed fingers I sketched what I could see of the landscape, and wrote a few lines in my notebook. Then, breasting the snow again, crossing the shifting avalanche slopes and torrents, I reached camp about dark, wet and weary and glad.

Muir came to mind as the sun made the bay much brighter and far less dreary for us. We hove to near the Marble Islands, passing icebergs that were white and translucent green. The islands are excellent rookeries, a center for sitting and circling birds: hundreds of phalaropes in the water; groups of pigeon guillemots, marked by white shoulders, floating near shore; tufted puffins, as bizarre in shape and appearance as any bird in Alaska, dashing with a flash of orange and black out across the water and among the icebergs.

What colors! The water was pale blue green. Some of the neighboring icebergs were laden with birds, even bald eagles. The brilliant lavender, both of fireweed and of the feet of guillemots, met the brightness of the sun as it began to break through the mist.

On our approach to the islands we heard the constant shouting, screaming, chattering, and calling of the birds, in every cadence and pitch. It was as though we had come to the stirring final movement of a concerto.

Glaucous-winged gulls took the place of violins. Soloists rose and sang their arias briefly, after which they soared to the rocks to rest. A gentle lapping of water against the shore sounded like the tinkle of bells and the light roll of drums. All this harmony seemed to impart a stability and rhythm where nothing is stable and there is only the indefinable rhythm of the universe.

Yet nothing was hectic. The free and natural movement of organisms manifested itself with elegant simplicity. To punctuate this thought three black pelagic cormorants peeled from the sloping rocks and swooped in a graceful arc down to

GLACIER BAY
NATIONAL MONUMENT, ALASKA:
top–stranded iceberg at Reid Inlet;
bottom–harbor seal basking in Muir Inlet;
right–Muir Glacier

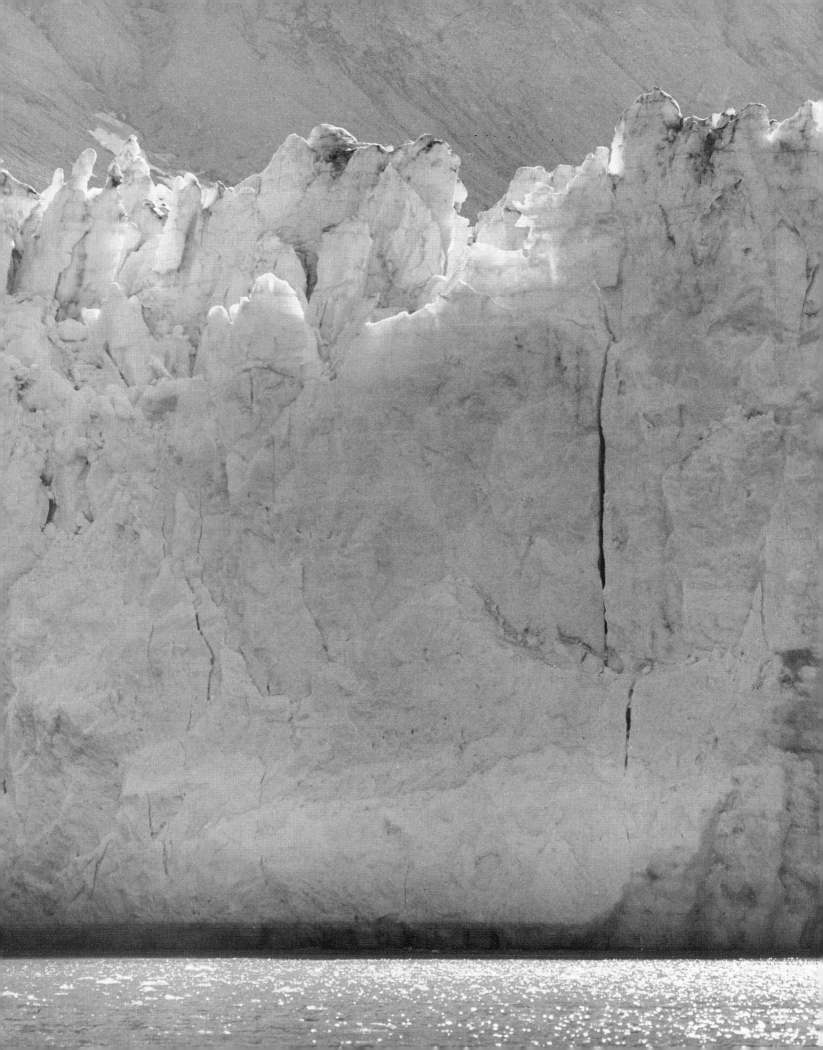

the water surface, there to skim above it and disappear as specks in the distance.

On leaving the Marble Islands we were observed by seals, rising at different points around us. Killer whales surfaced and spouted. Porpoises leaped in pairs. Hundreds of scoters blackened the water as they flew over. We stopped on shore for a break, noting tracks of coyotes, wolves, and bears.

Coming out of Sandy Cove we got a magnificent view of the Fairweather Range, its highest summit reaching to more than 15,000 feet, clear of clouds, shining white and dazzling against the sky.

From hidden cirque lakes high up on the peaks came ribbons of water, plunging down cliffs and tumbling over talus to get to the sea. On the shoulder of Mount Wright, mountain goats perched on precipitous cliffs.

John Muir built a cabin in 1890 to facilitate studies of glaciers, but all that remains at the site today is an inconspicuous pile of rocks and a grove of alders 20 feet high. How strange it suddenly seemed that all was barren here in Muir's time. The site had then been barely uncovered by the melting and receding Muir Glacier. Now the front has retreated 20 miles and is still receding.

The forest now sheltering the cabin site is composed of alder with red-berried elder, foamflower, dwarf fireweed, moss, grass, and ferns. It is a more primitive forest than that of the Sitka spruce and hemlock at the mouth of the bay, where the ice has been gone for nearly two centuries.

At the Muir cabin site the land has been free of ice for not even a single century and the forest has barely reached a stage of adolescence. As we went farther up the bay, the forest gradually diminished until at last there was nothing but a mat of herbs and lichens. Beyond was barren ground and finally solid ice.

It is clear from this that one type of vegetal growth succeeds another after the ice retreats. As a classical sequence of glacial retreat and ecological succession, Glacier Bay in its natural state is priceless.

The Institute of Polar Studies says Muir Inlet "offers an unparalleled opportunity for studies of soil development and repopulation by plants and animals in a recently deglaciated area.... Glacier Bay is unique because nowhere else in the world are there glaciers retreating with such rapidity that have been so well studied and for which the rate of retreat and positions for given dates are so accurately known. Although most of this retreat has been in sea water, sizeable tracts of land which were freed from ice within a short span of time have well-defined habitat types representing successional stages, from the barren ice front to mature forest."

Since 1959 the institute has been systematically studying the glacial geology of the area so that the history of the dwindling ice is well cataloged. A fascinating bit of information uncovered is that with the slowly warming climatic trend and consequent release of the great ice load from the land, the shores of Glacier Bay are emerging from the sea at a rate of over four centimeters per year.

With the maritime climate of moderate temperatures and heavy rainfall, plant growth in Glacier Bay is bound to be vigorous. In the early pioneer stage comes avens (*Dryas drummondi*), a matted, yellow-flowered member of the rose family that sows its seeds on the wind. The seeds of willow get lodged in these mats, and horsetails (*Equisetum*) start to grow in ponds. The sequence goes on from there: open thicket, closed thicket, emergence of cottonwood over alder, then spruce, and finally a mixed spruce-hemlock forest growing from a luxuriant floor festooned with twayblade, an orchid. This cycle can be completed in less than a century and it does not take much longer than that for the litter on the forest floor to reach a thickness of 20 centimeters.

It is simply a succession of one ecosystem after another. Near the fronts of melting glaciers, where there is least vegetation, snow buntings and rock ptarmigans find an environment to their liking. At the opposite extreme—in the mature spruce-hemlock forests—live chestnut-backed chickadees, thrushes, and pine grosbeaks.

Insects, such as plant lice, appear as soon as plants appear. Then come beetles, thrips, bees, spiders, and others as the community expands and each species occupies its niche.

It takes about 25 years before mammals move in to occupy deglaciated areas, since all are dependent directly or indirectly on plants for cover or food or both. The first to appear are wandering shrews and deer mice. With the advance of marshy, grassy, and forested environments, the community is enlarged by such immigrants as voles, squirrels, and martens. Larger and more peripatetic species—mountain goats, wolves, seals, and porpoises—move into their own preferred habitats.

And yet, above all else, are the transcendent mysteries of the glaciers: Why, when it took a thousand years for the last ice to invade this area and cover it to a depth of several thousand feet and then stay there for a thousand years, has melting now proceeded so rapidly? Why has the region literally been uncovered in only a single century? The rate of retreat here is said to be 15 times as fast as that of most glaciers elsewhere in the world.

We moved deeper into this raw and rugged land. The bays grew narrower. The waters changed from blue green to a light milky green, the result of suspended sediment poured into the bay by silt-laden glacial streams. In places the water was as smooth as glass, reflecting sharp-edged snowy peaks.

The melting remnants of icebergs occurred in every conceivable shape and form, some jagged, some statuesque with deep blue eyes and ivory arms, some perforated with holes or designed with alcoves; others looked like logs or rafts and had birds sitting on them in rows.

Why the ice was blue in places and white in others struck us as an interesting optical phenomenon. When an iceberg breaks or cracks to expose deep crevasses where the ice is fresh, the crystals act as prisms to refract blue light and absorb other colors. On overcast days the blue becomes especially intense because more of it penetrates the clouds than any other color. On exposure of ice to air, small bubbles form between the crystals, after which all colors of light are refracted and the ice appears white to our eyes.

Past Geikie Inlet we seemed surrounded by snow-laden peaks, and we felt we had entered a world of blue and white. John Muir spoke of "myriads of minute and intensely brilliant radiant lights burning in rows on the banks of streams and pools and lakelets from the tips of crystals melting in the sun, making them look as if bordered with diamonds. These gems are rayed like stars and twinkle; no diamond radiates keener or more brilliant light. It was perfectly glorious to think of this divine light burning over all this vast crystal sea in such ineffably fine effulgence, and over how many other of icy Alaska's glaciers where nobody sees it."

On the other hand, a variety of color was there if we sought it. Seals rested on shore among the rocks. Sheer cliffs of yellow and brown came down to meet the milky green water. Up some V-shaped side valleys we saw localities that looked like Yellowstone Canyon, and some that resembled badlands.

The forests vanished. The percentage of barren gray rock increased. The water became either beige or brown.

At this point, glaciers filled nearly every cove, every inlet, every mountain valley. So much moisture had moved into this humid coastal area over the millennia and risen and fallen as snow or freezing ice that some of the largest glaciers in Alaska had formed. Glacier Bay and vicinity, with more than 16 active tidewater glaciers, became an extraordinary assemblage.

We could not possibly see everything at once. We were overwhelmed. Ice came down the mountains, coalesced in the valleys, and approached the sea in massive floes. Every kind of glacial feature was being formed—medial moraines, lateral moraines, terminal moraines, ice falls, crevasses, cliffs, tunnels, terraces, platforms, bridges, grooves, layers of icebound sediment, polished promontories. Talk about a geologist's paradise!

It was a long trip, close to a hundred miles the way we had come from Bartlett Cove. Persons who would like to come by plane or helicopter, or who think that an elegant lodge on a prominent point here would be just the thing, should reconsider.

The scene is so pure, so perfect, so exquisite that the hand of man but mars it. Indeed, the sound of the motor was an unforgivable intrusion. Ideally, the way to get the feel of this bay would be to come in by canoe, camping in secret coves along the way. Weather and waves, however, can make that trip exceedingly perilous for any but experienced boatmen.

In any case, by boat you come in slowly, and the changing scenes pervade your senses during the day with mind-enlarging, exhilarating vistas. The brain is bathed and relaxed by the fundamental peace and beauty of this bay. You do not see these views all at once, as an aircraft would thrust them upon you. They come in bits and pieces. You savor each shape of iceberg, every cloud, every color of flower and frozen cliff. One at a time the fantasy-filled panoramas are revealed. You live in a succession of changing worlds.

And suddenly you realize that you are living more lives than one.

We wanted to reflect on this, but at that moment we passed an iceberg that looked like a jet aircraft that had come sliding to a halt in the water.

As we approached Johns Hopkins Inlet the landscape became overwhelming in its brightness and fascinating in its shades of blue and purple, an unfolding pageant that had no end. Cascades came down for thousands of feet to join the sea. Up on the crags some glaciers perched precariously and we could imagine the crashing clatter when a chunk broke off and fell a thousand feet to the talus below.

Brown patches remained where erosion had brought down sediments from loftier sites and deposited them on the ice.

There was so much to see that a hundred entries into this wild domain would have been insufficient to capture each color, discern every nuance of nature, or absorb all the sights and sounds. The icebergs alone presented to the eye an immense and refreshing array of forms and designs. Some were only a foot or so above the water. Some were clean, others filled with gravel. A few were pierced with holes or sharpened into knifelike blades by gradual melting.

One was a chicken sitting on the water. Another was an anvil. There were many T-shaped forms. And bridges, pinnacles, obelisks, upturned goblets, swans, ships, sails. There were never two forms alike. The human imagination is constantly captured and held by such an endless range of variations.

Some icebergs had geometric, angular designs on one side and on the other, delicate lacelike work supported on skimpy superstructure. The top-heavy pieces would either roll over in the next few hours or break and spill their upper parts into the water. Now and then we saw icebergs roll over as melting changed the balance of weight.

Everything was wet and melting. The days had 22 hours of light and the warmth abided also for that extended period.

Rounding the corner into Johns Hopkins Inlet we saw the head of the bay, a culmination of soaring, sharp-pointed peaks aglow with ice.

For a while we stopped and floated in silence. But there was no silence! The roar of waterfalls plunging over glacial boulders and discharging their muddy torrents into the sea came from both sides of the inlet. John Muir called them a choir of cascades chanting rain songs.

We heard the lapping of water beneath the icebergs, and an inexplicable popping as wavelets poked into pockets of ice and out again.

From afar came the constant rumbling and grinding of glaciers as they slowly, ponderously moved to the edge of the sea and crumbled. A resonant BOOM roared across the bay when each chunk calved and slid into the water with a flurry of spray.

The sound struck back and forth; simultaneously it seemed to come from above and below, as though the bay, the mountains, the sky—the whole earth —were a giant sounding board, or an echo chamber, where only the gods— or the gulls—were powerful enough to speak. John Muir wrote of the sound in his *Travels in Alaska:*

> When a large mass sinks from the upper fissured portion of the wall, there is first a keen, prolonged, thundering roar, which slowly subsides into a low muttering growl, followed by numerous smaller grating clashing sounds from the agitated bergs that dance in the waves about the newcomer as if in welcome; and these again are followed by the swash and roar of the waves that are raised and hurled up the beach against the moraines. But the largest and most beautiful of the bergs, instead of thus falling from the upper weathered portion of the wall, rise from the submerged portion with a still grander commotion, springing with tremendous voice and gestures nearly to the top of the wall, tons of water streaming like hair down their sides, plunging and rising again and again before they finally settle in perfect poise, free at last, after having formed part of the slow-crawling glacier for centuries.

Long after the fall a swell progresses down the inlet, comes up under projecting edges of other masses of ice, and in its succeeding movements orchestrates a musical interlude.

We passed an old mining camp, where we found evidence of early attempts to dig out gold, and were reminded that mining is legally possible yet in this area. In 1935, ten years after Glacier Bay was established as a national monument, the celebrated author Rex Beach, who had a friend among the miners here, persuaded another friend, Franklin D. Roosevelt, to open the monument to mining operations.

It is still open and at any time a road could scar those hills and violate the sanctuary and beauty that was meant to be preserved. Monument officials can only require that a prospective miner get permission to build a road or erect a building; they must painfully grant pro forma assistance in locating a road instead of denying it. The solution to this dilemma lies in making Glacier Bay a national park, an ultimate status for which it thoroughly qualifies.

At the mouth of Reid Inlet we went ashore with sleeping bags to spend the night in this magnificent wilderness. Of course, there was little night to speak of at 59° north latitude. The sun went down at eleven in one of those long Arctic sunsets that never really terminates and then turns into dawn at two or three in the morning.

There was little silence, either, and this was one of the reasons we wanted to spend a night alone in this environment: to hear its music, to listen to its voices, to get the subtle and delicate feeling that cannot be obtained by roaring down the bay in a motorboat.

Gulls greeted us as we stepped ashore. Arctic terns swirled around, setting up a welcome or a warning and wheeling over toward Reid Glacier, which looked so near but still lay two or three miles away.

En route to the camp we passed a singing stream of clear water that fell from a cliff and broke into many channels as it made its way to the sea.

Every once in a while the gentle music was interrupted by the boom of a calving berg. Each time we looked in vain to see the fall, but the sight had come and gone long before the sound arrived. We looked toward the glacier. All lay quiet except for gulls wheeling over the worried waters.

Around us in the purple evening glow rose regal peaks in all directions, softened by haze. Beneath them, like the coils of sailors' ropes, curved the outlines of the great snowfields. Ice drifted out into the bay; here and there on shore a few chunks lay at random, stranded, scattered, ghostlike in the twilight, almost grotesque in their multiple shapes, awaiting the rise of tide to float again.

A breeze arose, underscoring the high-pitched chatter of terns. The cries of gulls sounded forlorn in the shadows.

Among the rocks at the water's edge walked a black oyster catcher, a heavy-bodied shore bird with pale pink legs and spearlike orange beak. It sounded a steady peeping that mingled with the tinkling of water against the dull gray rocks. Somewhere within those rocks the bird may have had a nest, which would most likely have been a mosaic of small rock chips so artfully camouflaged as to be nearly impossible to find. This species has evolved a clever ability not only to lure intruders away from its nest, but also to build a decoy nest.

There would not seem to be much food for wildlife here, but oyster catch-ers manage to find enough in the water to sustain themselves: not oysters, but related mollusks such as mussels, or crustaceans such as barnacles, or perhaps a marine worm when available.

All night the booming sounded from the face of the distant glacier. Echoes came and went with eerie celestial overtones, like thunder without a storm, un-familiar, unreal, somehow attuned to an unfathomable metaphysical world about which man knows little.

Indeed the breaking of the ice represents a cosmic cycle of some unknown dimension. It is a cycle that gives to the earth long-range pulsations of climate which sometimes cause the glaciers to advance or, as now, to rumble and break as they melt. We are witness to a grand but cryptic message from the universe, a message of time and rhythm and creation that is as yet ill-defined by men. But it is there. We perceive and wonder—and hope that sometime man will know.

Next morning we walked along the shore and photographed the crystalline sculpture of the stranded bergs and then took off by boat to Margerie Glacier. We moved in close (but not too close) to the blue white wall of ice, from which great chunks crashed now and then. Each time this happened, providing the mass of ice was large enough, the water surged and the swell clacked floating chunks together. This sound spread all around us, stereo fashion, and tapered away as the waves went down the bay.

Black-legged kittiwakes, a kind of gull, sped to the scene and often dived into the water for bits of life that the plunging iceberg impelled to the surface.

At one side, next to the glacier front, a colony of kittiwakes clung to the cliff, their nests attached to the merest ledges, the gray and white young serene-ly watching the world from what seemed highly precarious perches. True to their custom the gulls collected over the boat as we floated silently by, voicing their protest at our intrusion but at the same time taking careful advantage of mor-sels we might have stirred to the surface.

The raucous calls formed a collection of deafening sounds and musical themes. We taped them on the spot, about a hundred at once, and have played the recording often; few things better recall the wilderness than its voices.

Kittiwakes spend the greater part of their lives far out to sea, but when they come ashore to nest they gather in noisy clusters and their soliloquies take many forms: clipped notes in various keys, wide-mouthed screeches, plaintive shouts, chipping pips, a hoarse and rhythmic "kittiwake-kittiwake-kittiwake."

It was a long way from Tarr Inlet to Muir Inlet, but we could tell upon arrival that twice the trip would have been worth the trouble. The front of Muir Glacier was a sculpture gallery of celestial proportions. The sun's rays came in low, painting an afternoon glow on sharp-pointed pinnacles, aquamarine crevasses, serrated crests, and sheer ice cliffs with an infinite range of designs.

Hundreds of harbor seals lay on the floating ice cakes that filled the bay. Sunning themselves, sleeping, cradling their young, rolling off their wet white rafts to plunge for food, some of them looked like bewhiskered sea captains adrift in bathtubs.

Questions flooded our thoughts: What food do the seals eat and where does it come from? With so many seals here—all obviously comfortable and satisfied with life—there must be something to attract them. The streams coming fresh from glaciers could hardly carry much food. Even in summer the water at the surface of the bay is less than 50 degrees in temperature, and doubtless is colder farther below. Yet Arctic waters often are richer in nutrients than tropic waters, so we are left with little in the way of answers to our questions. Man's research has only begun. We can suppose only that this ecosystem functions as efficiently as any other.

There is, to be sure, a great deal yet to be learned, not only about the delicate interrelationships among organisms—terrestrial, aerial, and marine—but also about how human beings should manage so huge and diverse an area. We talked about this at considerable length with Monument Superintendent Robert Howe, an experienced biologist, and his staff, all competent to the last man, well trained, and as dedicated to their work (understandably!) as any men we know.

Glacier Bay National Monument consists of 4,400 square miles—it is much larger than Yellowstone National Park—and offers an abundance of challenges.

People, for example. Despite the difficulties of getting to Glacier Bay, it is not very secret any more. The monument already has over 5,000 visitors per year, and the number is increasing annually.

Ninety percent of all tourists arrive by air. A few retired people in large boats (which are safer than small ones) spend time exploring the western coast of Alaska, though they are reluctant to expose their boats to icebergs.

A limited supply of comfortable housing and good food is available at park headquarters, and visitors may go out into the bay on all-day excursions aboard large, well-equipped tour boats—luncheon and explanations of passing features are included.

There are other ways to enter this ice-filled wilderness, one of which is especially recommended by monument officials, though not for everyone: Go out and be left at some secluded point or hidden cove, spend the night in the wilderness, and be picked up a day or more later. Obviously this calls for maximum self-reliance on the part of the backcountry camper. He has no help once the boat that brought him goes away. He must know how to conduct himself and he must have adequate food, survival gear, warm clothing, and sleeping equipment. He carries out every scrap of his own trash, leaving only footprints behind. He must know what to do (and what not to do) if he meets a grizzly (weighing up to a thousand pounds). He can carry no gun; he is a visitor, not a master. Parks, as the saying goes, are for animals.

Though Glacier Bay may seem far away from the bustling crowd, laws and law enforcement are always there, and they stem from multiple sources.

The United States Coast Guard claims jurisdiction over the water in the area. The Alaska Fish and Game Department has jurisdiction over all fisheries. Alaska state troopers take care of felonies committed. Ordinary public safety is relatively easy to manage, but aerial searches and elaborate rescues may require far more facilities than the National Park Service has, and communications may be poor when needed most. Thus all persons entering the monument and desiring to disappear into the wilderness should leave with park rangers their planned itineraries and time of intended return. This narrows the radius of search, if search there must be, and gives the rangers a starting point: Anyone 24 hours overdue becomes an object of attention.

In Glacier Bay, a great deal of snow falls, but the temperature rarely gets very far below zero. Highest temperatures in summer go only into the seventies.

Much salmon (all species) and halibut are taken commercially, and there is bound to be some pollution from careless fishermen. Salmon are sometimes fished intensively, too, outside the bay, but little is known as to what effect this has on the marine habitat within the bay.

The trouble is that ecosystems here are naturally changing so rapidly that funding of research (which Congress traditionally guards with care) cannot keep pace, or at least has not kept pace. To map, photograph, survey, assess, analyze —all these activities take time and effort and appropriations, and unless there are more of all these the superintendent is unaware of what he has to manage, and what is happening to Glacier Bay. With such priceless real estate it seems unwise to take any chances.

As for natural and unexpected hazards, earthquakes sometimes cause a good deal of excitement. The Fairweather fault, a sizeable fracture in the crust of the earth, extends beneath a portion of the monument and has gone on a rampage. Movement along it triggered an earthquake on July 9, 1958, releasing 90 million tons of rock that fell into Lituya Bay. The rockslide, plunging into one side of a narrow inlet, forced water on the other side to surge up and out in what has been called the biggest splash in history. Water rose up to 1,720 feet on the side of a mountain slope and in just a few seconds trimmed off soil and forest as smoothly as if the slope had been polished by glaciation.

The wave then surged out into the bay and thence to the sea, wiping out a boat, two lives, and many more acres of forest along the shore. It was eight times higher than any seismic sea wave (tsunami) ever recorded.

Even without earthquakes, Lituya Bay is a place of action. It has such a narrow entrance that tides rip in and out like waterfalls, and in that extremely dangerous situation many a life has been lost. This can be very difficult country for the uninitiated, as the French explorer La Perouse discovered in 1786. He lost 21 men at the entrance to this bay.

Nowadays rangers try to forestall boating accidents by advising all who enter Glacier Bay of the hazards. There are always icebergs, and frequently rain and fog, in the bay.

In some places tidal currents in excess of five knots are common. Severe whirlpools may be encountered. Into such areas the National Park Service cautions that only boats equipped with radar should make any attempt at passage in foggy weather.

Reefs are also a hazard. And so, perhaps, is the drinking water that boatmen sometimes pull ashore to seek: Some of the streams in Johns Hopkins Inlet, for example, are reported to contain arsenic, presumably from arsenic-bearing rocks.

Still, it is icebergs that can cause the most trouble. They fall from glacier fronts, or unexpectedly shoot up out of the bay, or roll over without warning. When conditions are right, they may travel at four knots. Icebergs drifting into Anchorage Cove have been known to foul anchor chains and dislodge anchors; in a matter of hours icebergs can collect and prevent a boat's departure for days.

In this wildlife sanctuary, poaching is not a severe problem. Fishermen sometimes shoot from boats, which is more on the order of vandalism than poaching; they may engage in a kind of random target practice to see if they can hit whatever is moving on shore. Such is the case with the fisherman's revenge against lounging seals, for seals at times take bites out of commercial catches as they are being hauled aboard fishing vessels. In fact, some fishermen will just about shoot anything they think eats fish.

Probably the greatest long-range challenge to human management of Glacier Bay, however, is the exclusion of lodges, roads, tramways, and similar disturbances of urbanization. Such things have been wished on pristine areas before, by both federal officials and conservationists. Today, the measure of maturity in any nation is its degree of restraint in handling natural resources. In such an environment as Glacier Bay, man should not be a wild and noisy intruder, bringing his homes and motors with him, but rather a quiet one who comes for a while and then departs without a trace.

*　　*　　*

We headed back toward Bartlett Cove as the sun went down. It was almost midnight. The final rays of light had turned to reddish purple the peaks that lay along a ridge to the east. It was an alpenglow, a "celestial amethystine light," as John Muir would have called it, that lasted for an hour or so in the long sub-Arctic twilight.

The memory of Glacier Bay would last much longer than an hour or a day or a decade. The land and its cosmic rhythms were too big to understand—or forget—very easily. Of our secret places, it was the largest, the grandest in scope, and possibly the most mysterious.

When man resolves some more of the riddles of this endlessly fascinating bay, with its ice and mountains and wildlife, it may be that he will have revealed a few of the secrets of time, the earth, the universe—and perhaps himself.

Lava Beds, California 🦋

THEY LOOK LIKE HADES CONGEALED. CAULDRONS ONCE HOT and exploding now lie cold and lifeless. Fountains of fire have subsided. Lava once glowing with incandescence has covered the land in a chaotic jumble of black and gray.

One's first impression is that this is not much to inspire exuberance. Spanish explorers in the Old Southwest considered lava beds splendid terrain to avoid. Here in the Northwest, life on lava was only for Indians rugged enough to endure it, and even the climate contrived to turn men back. The temperature varies from well below zero in winter to over a hundred degrees in summer. The annual precipitation is 13 inches, a desert quota. What rain there is evaporates or sinks into porous lava fields and drains away; there are no lakes, no ponds, no streams.

Thus the traveler en route to the Lava Beds has, to all appearances, little hope of making exciting discoveries, and as a result he plans to move on after stopping briefly.

And so what follows will serve him right. His sequence of errors commences with poor advance planning and poor research.

Our first visit to the Lava Beds ended in vexation, and with a resolve to return for much longer exploration. We have since returned, but have not yet done the job right. That would take years. We have left less done than undone because the Lava Beds hold more secrets than any textbook or brochure reveals.

One revelation: The region contains almost as great an accumulation of volcanic phenomena as the Hawaiian Islands. The whole Cascade Range has been active for a long time, and flows of tuff and lava have issued in this particular corner of what is now California for the past 35 million years.

On approaching the Lava Beds the road traverses deep canyons and broad fields of red and black rock, then rises upward to 5,000 feet in elevation and enters a land of ponderosa pine and sagebrush. Pure black dunes, composed of cinders that hardened after being expelled from a volcanic vent and blown some distance away, give to the scene a mystic, photo-negative quality; in this landscape black and white are reversed.

The terrain is cut by numerous faults, zones of weakness through which the inner contents of the earth had easy access to the surface. Flow after flow has come from deep-seated sources, overlapping each other and piling up thickly across the land.

The oldest flow now visible in Lava Beds National Monument, a preserve of about 72 square miles set aside for the public in 1925, is 60,000 years in age, and the youngest flow is about 500 years old.

The Lava Beds may look cold and quiet now, but fire and brimstone were the order of their day. By the evidence remaining, it is clear that incandescent molten rock often seethed through earth cracks and burst into elongated lava fountains, or "curtains of fire." Where pools of lava bubbled and splattered in relative quiet, they built up spatter cones.

Exploding gas, under high pressure, tossed out globs of lava, which left behind frothy, jagged piles of red or black rock with a colorful sheen. It is not unlike piles of fudge just poured into a pan and not yet smoothed.

Sometimes the molten rock oozed out and cooled into fingers of taffylike lava called pahoehoe (a Hawaiian term pronounced *pah-ho-ay-ho-ay*). At other times it hardened and collected in chunks and was pushed from behind into a sharp-edged jumble called aa (pronounced *ah-ah*). Pumice, a lightweight froth, gathered on molten pools. Block lava and bombs were hurled from exploding vents. An outcrop of obsidian, volcanic material that cooled into a glasslike texture, is also found in the Lava Beds.

Because of this fiery and flaming past, the northeast corner of California is covered with cinder, spatter, and driblet cones; deep fissures; pits; caves; and flows that cover thousands of square miles.

The land is neither flat nor simple, and has certainly had a lively history, biologically as well as geologically. Some of the lava pits contain remains of native camels and mastodons that used to roam the wilds of North America. No sooner had the flows cooled than various organisms ventured upon them and today all kinds of life survive where once was only burning, flaming, eruptive violence.

A pinkish light spreads across the sky at dawn and moves into the ragged, shadowed valleys. A haze, hanging over the lower gullies, blurs the outlines of the lava. Swallows fly in and out among the Sierra junipers. A chipmunk climbs to the upper branches of bitterbrush. A quail calls from a hidden post.

The sun comes up as a flattened globe, deep orange in color, enlarging as though a flood of lava were coming. Its rays strike the edges of lava and the tips of leaves. From the crags on Schonchin Butte the morning song of the canyon wren sounds like some celestial flute. Cottontails and jackrabbits move about. The daytime community is awakening, while nocturnal creatures withdraw to their burrows or roosts.

Cinder cones and lava bluffs rise from the haze as shadowy islands in a diaphanous sea. Taller trees atop the buttes or in the highlands receive the sun with royal grace.

We hiked one morning in the region of Eagle Nest Butte, where the golden trunks of ponderosa pine looked much like marble columns on old Roman streets in the Middle East. It was not too early for the birds to sing, nor for chipmunks and squirrels to hustle at furious speed on the fallen logs. A woodpecker's pounding came through the woods like the tattoo of a distant drummer.

How fresh the air was! It held a dozen aromas, among which the human scent organs are barely able to distinguish. There was pine, juniper, sagebrush, the dankness of morning dew on decaying needles, the earthy odors of dust that had begun to circulate through the air with the stirrings of man and beast.

And what music! The wheezing note of the towhee was too high in pitch and far too fast for us to determine what the bird was saying in its stepped-up world, but we taped the song and played it back at a speed one-eighth as fast. This brought the notes and nuances down to a level at which we could hear and separate them. They had a gurgling quality, opened by a note that sounds like a blast from three trumpets. The precision of interval between each note suggests a voice apparatus precisely honed; it is able to rattle off 28 notes in half a second.

With 200 species of birds listed as living in the Lava Beds region, there is usually an abundance of sound that can be heard. Another rattling, buzzing call came from the high-flying nighthawk. The mourning dove issued its call from an old dead limb. Ash-throated flycatchers chirped in the top of a juniper. A morning breeze began to rise, adding to the sounds of life the sigh of wind through the needles. And there were also the strange sounds and notes and warnings from species of animals with which we were unfamiliar.

We came to a ponderous, jagged lava flow 20 feet in height. So recently had it issued from the earth that not even a fern-bush seed had begun to sprout. But even though it was black and lifeless, the flow lacked nothing in offerings of form or shape for the perceptive artist. Great plunging crevasses, arranged in a steplike pattern, fell where the molten crust had cracked in a dozen places as it cooled, hardened, and fell over the lip of a slaggy pile.

The plastic lava squeezed upward and sideways into an infinite number of pinnacles, obelisks, peaks, and mounds, like a garden of statues, all in black. Saw-toothed edges formed when gases within the lava exploded. Pits and vesicles remained where the gas once was. Congealed and cold, the lava lay crumpled, twisted, folded, and bent. Some was poured, some pushed, some crushed between opposing forces. There were archways, caves, bluffs, and chaotic crags.

We walked at times on a mat of pine needles, attempting to miss the abundant cones that were scattered so widely. In places a little erosion as well as vegetation had begun to reduce the fresh lava flows to soil. And finally, on the barren black rocks, a fern-bush had managed to gain a roothold. Though small and somewhat stunted, it was thriving nevertheless. This member of the rose family, with its fragrant flowers of yellow and white, is a ubiquitous plant in

LAVA BEDS
NATIONAL MONUMENT, CALIFORNIA:
top–Devils Homestead Lava Flow;
bottom–swallowtail butterfly;
right–pictographs in Fern Cave

the West and obviously hardy. Here it survived on minimum water and soil.

Wherever we looked our eyes were captured by some compelling evidence of a world in motion. An old toppled pine log, victim of the high prairie winds that sweep through here from time to time, held in the clutch of its roots a bushel of boulders. The wood itself had begun to decay, helped along by insects.

At times the forest closed in thickly around the trail, and we walked through cloisters of mountain mahogany—another distinguished member of the rose family. Little had we realized that so many roses could flourish so widely in a country solid with black lava and cinder dunes.

In places the dark forest floor was brightened with bracteate red spikes of paintbrush, and with clumps of buckwheat and milfoil. Even the observant hiker, and less often the motorist, seldom sees these minute flowers that bloom very close to the ground. Their fragile and delicate beauty is not diminished by being so small; with a magnifying lens their wonders are revealed in surprising complexity.

On lava as well as on tundra, we were presented with treasures we did not expect, and with other reasons for wishing we could live additional lives: to enter the microcosm of minute plants and learn what effect they have in breaking down bare rock into usable soil; to study the life history and ecological influence of the fern-bush on these once barren beds, thus gaining some insight into the succession of life on newborn land; and to investigate the habits of sagebrush and its associated animal life.

Our path through the pines was covered with animal tracks, impressed in a springy white pumice. The holes of rodents and insects were a reminder that men see little of what goes on unless they stay for hours or days and remain as silent as possible.

Life moved all around us. A red-shafted flicker flew into the top of a dead ponderosa pine. Piñon jays swooped in pairs from tree to tree.

Coyotes are abundant on the Lava Beds. Bobcats are, too, with plenty of shelter and a good supply of rats, mice, and rabbits. The area is indeed a wildlife paradise. There would be more mammals if more water existed, but a mouthful of rodent is a mouthful of water, so that even without rain pools a substantial fauna exists.

Surprisingly, pronghorns live on the lava, where there seems to be too much broken terrain and too many holes to permit the kind of getaway speed these wary animals need. Here their pace could well be a breakneck speed—literally.

Efforts are under way to reintroduce bighorn sheep, which once roamed the buttes and flows. Mule deer are common, moving up to the highlands in summer and down in winter. Victor H. Cahalane, the distinguished biologist, tells of 26 deer that once fell on the ice at Tule Lake National Wildlife Refuge, north of the monument, and could not get up because it was too slippery.

"The men worked hard to drag them ashore," says Cahalane, "where they could get footing and dash away. One buck was very ungrateful, or more likely badly scared. After he had been brought ashore and had time to recover his composure and his breath, he arose to his feet and went after one of his rescuers. Quick-thinking, the man fled out on the lake. The deer chased him, fell down and had to be rescued all over again!"

We returned to camp at midmorning, dizzy with discovery, but immensely refreshed. The days were not long enough at the Lava Beds, so we used the nights as well, and went underground. There, we found that the nights were not long enough either.

The Lava Beds region is literally honeycombed—perhaps catacombed is a better word—with caves. Thanks to the central molten cores of certain lava masses that kept on flowing as the crust cooled off and hardened, there are hundreds of tubes that were emptied when the lava simply ran out from them.

It is as though the Lava Beds had a functional system of subway tunnels, crossing and crisscrossing, dipping and surfacing, intersecting, joining, branching, coalescing. Nearly 300 of these tubes have been found within the boundaries of the monument itself, and no one knows how many hundreds or thousands of others there are.

More than a hundred have been explored, though most are closed to visitors because of inherent dangers. Anyone wishing to enter a cave that is still undeveloped or unmaintained must obtain a written permit from monument headquarters. Applicants have to present satisfactory evidence of experience in spelunking, have proper equipment, and be in excellent physical condition.

About two dozen lava tubes have been developed and opened to the public.

All a visitor has to do is check out a gasoline lantern at headquarters and take off by himself, a technique calculated to bring out the explorer in anyone.

There are many entrances—Sentinel Cave, Sunshine Cave, Thunderbolt Cave, Mush Pot Cave—a visitor has only to choose. We selected the Golden Dome Cave, lighted our lantern, switched on a "Safari Lite," put flashlights in our pockets like six-shooters ready to draw in case we needed to illuminate something special with maximum wattage, and started downward.

If we expected a dreary, formless tube, we were fortunately mistaken, and soon discovered why. Descending a long, steep ladder, as though entering the blackest bowels of the earth, we discovered that the walls of these once hot tunnels had congealed into intricate shapes and forms.

The molten lava had slowed, become viscous, stopped, and hardened, and as the last of the little vesicles of gas exploded, the walls became rough and patterned. Dripping liquid rock transformed into "lava-cicles" on the sides and ceilings. Channels running with melted rock turned into terraces and tiny aqueducts. Canals ran parallel, coalesced, or hugged the walls. Some were deep and others were shallow. Some were straight and some were sinuous.

We moved ahead cautiously, trying to watch simultaneously where to put heads and feet. The lava was deceptive. We could not see it well in the flickering, dancing shadows. Depth and distance were hard to discern. In an absence of well-defined outlines it was hard to tell when we approached a lava-cicle and were about to connect with it sharply. Even with the light we had, very little of what was discernible stood out in a familiar way in this formless and shadowed void. We seemed to have lost the power of gauging dimension in that world of unreality where there were no dimensions.

Mark Twain described a "commodious tunnel" in Hawaii and told about lava-cicles in it. "The roof is lava, of course," he wrote in *Roughing It*, "and is thickly studded with little lava-pointed icicles an inch long, which hardened as they dripped. They project as closely together as the iron teeth of a corn sheller, and if one will stand up straight and walk any distance there, he can get his hair combed free of charge."

The floor of these tubes would be a delight to any sculptor, especially to those with fanciful insights on designs of tomorrow. In places we walked on virtually smooth and glassy surfaces, where the lava pools collected and slowly solidified without disturbance. In other places the lava had cracked while drying, opening crevices that made the footing tricky, or two streams had merged and forced up circular ridges that whirled in dizzy curlicues before solidifying.

Rapids. Currents. Eddy pools. Ripple marks. All the twisting motions of viscosity were there. It was easy to lose a foot in an unseen trough, or bark a shin on a ledge that was lost in shadow. But we could hardly take our eyes from the constantly changing forms on the floor. By moving the lantern we sent eerie shadows racing into the corners and brought forth from the path a new configuration of cracks and ridges.

On we went. The tube seemed to have no end. There were niches along the walls, as in burial chambers of ancient Rome. In places the roof had collapsed —or perhaps been blown out—and above could be seen a deep black sky full of stars.

Where two such collapses occurred in close proximity, the result was a natural bridge, of which at least 20 are known in this region. Sometimes the passage grew narrow, or the ceiling dipped so low that we had to scoot along on our haunches. At other times we came to chambers surprisingly colorful. In Golden Dome Cave some ceilings were coated with compounds of sulfur, which introduced into this somber place a cheerful mantle of yellow.

At length our eyes grew weighted with the burden of looking and seeing and marveling since dawn. We wanted to keep on the move, but if the mind remained elated at so many discoveries, the body commanded a halt to exploration and a climb out of the caves into the night—and bed.

But the next day there was a new surprise—unusually welcome because of the 100-degree heat that settled over the hazy summer landscape at midday.

This time we descended into Skull Cave, and no sooner had we dipped into the twilight of the entrance than we were bathed in cold air—much colder, it seemed, than the air of Golden Dome Cave had been—a luxurious atmosphere that seemed like walking into a chamber conditioned with refrigerated air.

The ceiling of Skull Cave seemed less tubelike than the others; it was larger, more jagged, uneven, vaultlike, coated with whitish rather than yellowish powder.

A few hundred steps to the back and then we clambered down over fallen rocks. The cave narrowed. Descending metal and wooden ladders we encountered deposits of ice and here the temperature fell toward freezing. At the bottom we stepped on a glassy surface of solid ice, thickness unknown. Under the glare of lights the ice seemed pure and clear, though a few boulders had fallen in the past and become embedded.

It was an unusual contrast, this chamber, once incandescent with heat, now deeply frozen.

More than a hundred caves in this area have been endowed with ice or water or both; at certain places, the ice is covered with a layer of water. In at least one instance, the ice looks like a giant, frozen waterfall, 20 feet high and 6 feet thick. Some frozen ponds, 400 feet long, look almost like rivers.

So well does the porous, vesicular lava insulate, that there is little heat exchange. The dense cool air of winter settles into the lowest chambers and pushes out any warmth that may have managed to get there. The ice itself is derived from rainwater percolating down through cracks and crevices.

Descent into the cold ice caves, an unexpected refreshment on a sweltering summer day, brought also the more intangible pleasures of the underground —quiet, stability, a sense of eternity, a feeling of peace.

But such a feeling has not always existed. With the coming of men there were eruptions other than lava ones.

Human beings have lived in this region for many years. The prehistoric village of Kumbat had 2,000 inhabitants, but little remains at the site today. North of Tule Lake is abundant evidence of early men: village sites, house sites, campsites, chipping stations, rock shelters, mortars, artwork, and graves.

In the Lava Beds one sees occasional pictographs on the walls of caves. These drawings, especially in Fern Cave, are elaborate, but have never been interpreted. The Indians who made them seem to have been nomadic, and little else than a few stone awls and obsidian chips attest to their presence.

In any case, the land was theirs until the 1800s; the first white men found Modoc Indians adapted to its topography, able to survive its vicissitudes. The newcomers rather liked the land, for all its hardships, and they increasingly invaded it. From the 1820s on, white men intermittently disturbed the streams and hunting grounds of the Modocs, fenced off meadows, and tried through trade and religious teachings to "civilize" the Indians. To a degree they succeeded: Modocs came to covet traders' goods and horses, unknown to them before.

The white men also brought smallpox; in the fall of 1847 this contagion killed nearly half the Modocs, including a considerable number of tribal elders and "wise men." That left hotheaded younger men to respond to the invasion.

Wagon trains poured out across the summer range of the Modocs and frightened away game animals upon which the Indians depended for food. It was a serious, deliberate blow, rather like a slow, invisible massacre, to which the Modocs responded under principles of primitive law, which was all they knew: Eliminate the marauders. Hence the Bloody Point Massacre of 1852, in which several wagon trains were ambushed by Modocs and many whites were killed.

The oncoming whites originated in a more lawful society, but now had left most of their laws behind. They killed. They massacred. They hunted Indians as they would deer. They brought the heinous practice of scalping.

And, of course, there were effective, successful tricks. At one point, the white Indian fighters invited the Modocs to a peace conference, cordially received 46 of them, then gunned down perhaps as many as 41.

The son of one of the slain men made every effort to halt the conflict. He was a Modoc Indian named Keintpoos, better known as Captain Jack. The white and the red could live in peace, he said, if only the whites (and it was a pathetic request) would give the Indians some land they could call their own.

The whites refused, insisting that the Modocs withdraw to a reservation in southern Oregon and share it with their deep, traditional, ancestral enemy, the Klamath Indians.

Captain Jack and his band tried twice to live there. Each time the Modocs were humiliated beyond endurance by the Klamaths and had to return to their own home ground.

In desperation, Captain Jack made a formal request to the commanding general of the Military Department of the Columbia for a small reservation along the Lost River. No action was taken.

Meanwhile, the inflooding settlers, harassed by Modocs, appealed to the United States Army for help, and on November 28, 1872, they got it—more or less. A patrol of troopers was sent out of Fort Klamath with orders to find the Modocs and place them back on the reservation—peaceably if possible, forcibly if need be.

On the following day the patrol rode into Captain Jack's camp on Lost River. All might have gone well had not one Indian refused to surrender his gun. An army lieutenant was ordered to take the weapon away from him, and that was the mistake that brought battle. Both men fired at about the same time, and thus began the most expensive and perhaps most bitter Indian war in which the United States Army was ever to engage.

Captain Jack and his followers withdrew into the Stronghold, a maze of jumbled black rock in the heart of the Lava Beds.

For two months the army assembled troops and volunteers, and in January 1873 the force closed in on the Lava Beds for what they thought would be an easy kill. The soldiers were confident, perhaps even arrogant, sure of driving the "ignorant savage" out of his lair. After all, they did outnumber the Indians by about 350 to 50.

Heavy fog lay over the lava that morning, and as the soldiers entered the rough, unfamiliar terrain, they saw no Indians and met no Indians—only the orange blast of gunfire, the scream of bullets, the shrieks of death.

The Indians were not confused. They knew exactly where to look and not be seen, how to hit and not be hit, to anticipate every enemy move, to cut off action, lay ambush, deceive, surround. . . . The army had walked into a trap of its own making.

By afternoon the fight was lost and the army retreated in failure, disorder, and disgrace. It had suffered 65 casualties, the Modocs none.

The troopers were impressed. They began to wonder whether even a thousand soldiers could dislodge any Modocs from the Stronghold.

Not that the Modocs were splendidly organized. It was just that the whites were less so. The army had been almost entirely demobilized after the Civil War, and what remained were mostly raw recruits. Out here they were learning quickly.

The army sought to negotiate. But the Indians, having won this battle, and being fully aware that the whites could not be trusted, refused.

By April the army had moved to the base of a nearby bluff—the action itself was somewhat of a bluff, a show of strength. Some distance away the soldiers set up a tent to which they hoped the Modocs would come to talk. They even named a peace committee to deal with the Modocs: Brig. Gen. E. R. S. Canby, friend of the Indians; A. B. Meacham, a civilian and also friend of the Indians; and a Methodist minister.

At this point the Indian attitude suddenly seemed to change. The Modocs requested a meeting in the tent, an unusual step that had all the marks of "Indian treachery." Indeed, the Modocs were not without guile; they knew the white man's ways, wore his clothes, fired his guns, spoke his language.

Forewarned, but unarmed, General Canby and his peace committee went to the tent, and in the midst of proceedings the general and the minister were slain. Meacham was shot three times and partially scalped, but he later recovered.

It was now clear to the army that the Stronghold must be taken, and a thousand angry soldiers stood ready to do so. Their orders were classic: "Exterminate the Modocs!"

Captain Jack still had only about 50 men, but the natural lava redoubts belonged to him, and their circuitous avenues were well known to his men.

This time the army troops moved in more slowly, from two directions instead of one, and stayed behind rock forts instead of retreating at night.

On the following day, forces from the east met forces from the west, after which the Modocs had no route to the water of Tule Lake, a short distance to the north. But the Indians continued to attack, and the battle went on.

By the third day Modoc defenders found their Stronghold nearly surrounded and the enemy still advancing. At that point, Captain Jack, before dawn on the morning of April 17, 1873, took his people—a total of 160 men, women, and children—through a trench that led to the south. With such silence did they depart that the soldiers knew nothing of the great escape until long after sunrise.

The army was now finally able to take over the Stronghold, at a cost that had risen to 85 casualties. The Indians had lost one man.

But the army had lost the Modocs, an embarrassing matter, and a search was ordered. Seventy men went out at dawn on April 26 to hunt near Schonchin Lava Flow. Their movements were watched, of course, and the Indians, seeing where they were headed, moved silently and invisibly to get there first.

From a high point with a commanding view the Modocs watched the soldiers arrive on the flat below. Then, surprised and not a little amused, they watched the soldiers gather together and stack their rifles, as on any parade ground. Many took off their shoes, sat down, and started eating lunch.

The Indians easily picked out their targets and opened fire. Twenty-seven soldiers perished. A few ran all the way back to base camp.

After a while the Indians, still amused, told the rest of the soldiers to go back home.

Captain Jack continued his retreat, moving from ice cave to ice cave in order to get enough water, and resigned to leaving the Lava Beds forever. But he and his band had a final chance to humiliate the United States Army, an opportunity he appreciated, for if the Modocs were to scatter they would need food, clothing, horses, and ammunition.

On the shore of Dry Lake the Modocs found and attacked another detachment. The soldiers panicked, as had the others, but this time they rallied, turned, and advanced. The Indians split and withdrew, once more eluding the army troops.

And yet, how long could such a meager band, however clever, hope to outlast the attackers?

On May 22, at the foot of Mount Dome, one group surrendered to the army. And they in turn led the troops to Willow Creek Canyon, where Captain Jack came out and lay down his arms.

He could not, he said, run any more.

With that the Modoc War came to an end. The leaders were taken back to the army camp, where ten gallows were erected. Revenge for the murder of General Canby and others would be swift, a lesson to any other tribes that wished to resist the whites.

This plan was rescinded by Washington, on the grounds that the executions could not take place without a trial. Even so, there seemed to be little spirit of equal justice for the Indians. At the court-martial, six Modocs were convicted and sentenced to death. President Grant commuted the sentences of two to life imprisonment, but on the morning of October 3, 1873, at Fort Klamath, the others were hanged—including Captain Jack.

53

All members of the Modoc tribe were there. They had been brought in by the army and forced to watch the death of their leaders. After that, the followers of Captain Jack were exiled to a reservation in Oklahoma.

This war, fought in the Lava Beds, cost the United States Army 143 casualties, including 68 dead. It involved over 1,200 regular army troops and cost the taxpayer somewhere between $500,000 and $5 million—all to defeat just 50 Indian braves.

Had the little reservation that Captain Jack sought on Lost River been given to the Modocs, it would have cost no more than $20,000.

* * *

Captain Jack's Stronghold remains today as it was when abandoned by the Modocs and the United States Army in 1873. Landmark sites of the battle are still undisturbed, and if while visiting there you wish to "separate from yourself," to recreate the battle in your own mind and try to understand it, and disappear from the present and go back to the time of the Modocs, you need only walk through the Stronghold.

The first part of the route is a trail formerly used by Indians in getting water from Tule Lake. Next, you come to a hidden shallow basin where soldiers camped in the Stronghold, then to crude stone walls erected by the attacking troops.

The summer sun beats down fiercely but is probably not much match for the hot time the Indians gave the soldiers.

The lava is far from barren, what with sagebrush, fern-bush, grass, and lichens, the last festooning the uneven landscape in shades of black, orange, gray, or chartreuse.

You enter Indian outposts, firing positions, and sentry caves, all with such excellent views of the terrain that you wonder how any foe could creep up undetected. Even if an enemy approached from the flank or rear he would have to rise over nearby ridges and expose himself to defensive fire. Just moving over this sharp and sometimes crumbly terrain is difficult enough.

The Stronghold was endowed, however, with natural "communications" trenches, defiles perhaps three feet wide and ten feet deep, through which the Modocs easily moved to and from their outposts.

54

You come to Captain Jack's command post, and here contemplate the course of battle not only for the Lava Beds, which were captured a hundred years ago, but for Indian peace and dignity, for which the struggle still goes on.

Emerging from the trenches you look into a cave, probably a collapsed lava tube, that sheltered a Modoc family during the war. Just beyond are low stone walls, which tempt you to surmise that the Modocs crept and crawled in order to keep from being seen.

Next is the Modoc council ground, a shallow depression where the Indians held councils of war, where they voted to continue the battle, and where they decided to murder the peace commissioners. Indeed, you can observe the very rock, a knob of lava, that Captain Jack used as a rostrum from which to plead with his followers not to kill the commissioners.

On either side you pass deep pits and areas of lava collapse. Then you enter another trench—the main line of Modoc defense.

But there are no Modocs. And no soldiers. Only birds and dragonflies, a deer now and then, and perhaps a few reticent rattlesnakes down below.

In the distance you can see Mount Shasta, nearly 50 miles away, softened by haze, its lower slopes blue, its coned white peak rising 14,162 feet into the California sky.

In the opposite direction lies Tule Lake itself, where at certain times of the year the greatest concentration of waterfowl in North America may be seen. Redhead ducks nest by the thousand, but in the autumn birds come by the million —pintails, mallards, widgeons, geese, and others. As many as five million pintails have assembled here. The site is well protected because Tule Lake National Wildlife Refuge, established in 1928, adjoins the northern boundary of Lava Beds National Monument.

The Lava Beds are being discovered by steadily increasing numbers of people, and there are now more than 100,000 visitors annually to Lava Beds National Monument. The campground is occupied every month, and some groups of people even come out to camp in the snow.

Many visitors find the cave trips tempting, and will obtain a lantern, or use their own sources of light, to enter and explore. Whether all these amateur speleologists come back out by nightfall is something on which park rangers have to keep tab. If at the end of the day all borrowed lanterns have not been returned, the ranger staff begins a search. Another way to determine whether anyone is trapped underground is to check parking areas: Any car remaining overnight at a cave parking area means a search of that cave for the owner of the car. Fire lookouts, able to view great expanses of the Lava Beds, are also instructed to watch for signs of visitors in trouble. But by and large few people get lost, and the problem is not a common one for rangers.

Professional speleologists take risks as a normal part of their work. One once broke his wrist in a lava cave. Another got stuck and could not get out by himself. Sometimes explorers have been plunged into blackness when the mantle of a lantern broke. The wiser explorers who run into trouble stay in one spot and rangers soon rescue them. The less wise ones crawl out, in pitch darkness, on hands and knees.

But risks or not, the rangers like to see cave exploration going on. "We feel that this is one park," said Superintendent Joe Kennedy, "where we offer visitors a unique national park experience by letting them take a lantern and go into these caves by themselves. It is a little bit of what the old-timers used to have when they started off into the unknown."

Kennedy says the park has had the usual share of vandalism, but he and his rangers have had remarkably good success in capturing those responsible.

Other problems are special and occasionally ominous. A few days before Easter one year a San Francisco radio station reporter called Kennedy on the telephone and asked if a group of persons would be permitted to come to the monument and practice guerrilla warfare.

Kennedy was somewhat surprised by such an unusual request, but had no doubt about answering it.

"Of course not," he replied. "Why?"

"Well, we have word that a group from San Francisco State College is planning to come up there this weekend and we'd like to get your thoughts about it."

"Okay. What do you want to know?"

"Would you allow a group to enter your area and undertake maneuvers?"

"Absolutely not."

"Would you allow people to go there and fire weapons?"

"We would not."

"How would you stop it?"

"We would get some of our men together and, well, we just wouldn't permit it."

"How many men do you have?"

"Enough."

What Kennedy meant was that if resources at the monument were insufficient, a call to the sheriff of Siskiyou County would have been in order.

Joe did call the sheriff and talked the matter over. He asked how many men the sheriff could place at his disposal.

"Several hundred if you need them," the sheriff answered.

As it happened, plans for such a trek were underway, and some quasi-guerrillas started out. The Forest Service was alerted to watch for them before they reached the Lava Beds. But they never arrived, for still unknown reasons.

To be sure, a certain freedom of action and spirit is encouraged in such wilderness areas as the Lava Beds. The pursuit thereof, however, must do no injury to other visitors or disturb their search for adventure, inspiration, and quiet.

* * *

Before leaving the Lava Beds, a visitor should know them by night. The moon spreads its light and fractures the shadows that lie over the black landscape. Flickering lights beyond Tule Lake are a measure of civilization too distant to seem relevant.

Sage-scented winds descend from the Medicine Lake highlands to cool and temper the day's heat that rises from the Lava Beds, and to sway the glinting tassels of mountain mahogany. The constellation Cassiopeia rises to the northeast. The Dipper swings in its arc down toward the Klamath lakes. The Northern Cross climbs overhead and Vega is at the zenith.

Perhaps it was on such a night that Captain Jack led his band from the Stronghold to take up new positions among the lava hills, en route out of their homeland forever.

The bark of a coyote comes from the canyon at our right. When it has echoed to the farthest buttes and flows, and when the final phrases have faded, there is a moment of silence in which our thoughts collide upon themselves and we realize how full of life and music and beauty this region is, and also how mysterious and little known.

Clarence King, the nineteenth-century geologist, spoke with a special insight when he described the Lava Beds as seen from the summit of Shasta. "I never tire of overlooking these great wide fields," he wrote, "studying their rich variety, and giving myself up to the expansion which is the instant and lasting reward. In presence of these vast spaces and all but unbounded outlook, the hours hurry by with singular swiftness. . . .

"Then, as you come again into softer air, and enter the comforting presence of trees, and feel the grass under your feet, one fetter after another seems to unbind from your soul, leaving it free, joyous, grateful!"

Place of Refuge, Hawaii 🍃

IF YOU HAPPENED TO BE HOTLY PURSUED BY YOUR ENEMIES, or had broken some taboo—here in the Hawaiian Islands the ancient system of what to do and what not to do was called the kapu—and you wanted to escape so as to try again some other day, you had only to reach a place of refuge, a pu'uhonua.

Once there you were safe. No one could enter the sacred precincts and pull you out. No one could besiege you and wait for you to emerge. There were no iron bars or armies to protect the place, yet you were utterly safe. In due course you could leave, and the protection of the pu'uhonua went with you.

As might be expected, the benefits of such an attractive arrangement were frequently taken advantage of. The Place of Refuge at Honaunau, on the island of Hawaii, gave sanctuary to countless harassed and troubled Hawaiians, and to-day, as the City of Refuge National Historical Park, it stands as a strange and lonesome outpost of a way of life gone by.

This sacred shelter by the sea was established at least six centuries ago, although no evidence remains to say precisely when. Similar refuges existed on other Hawaiian islands, but this one was apparently the most important. It is certainly the most visible and best preserved.

The Place of Refuge, as it is more commonly known, lies on a finger of ebony lava thrusting into the deep blue sea from the western coast of the island of Hawaii. It is outlined in white by foaming breakers that gently wash the shore. Seen from a vantage point on volcanic slopes above, surrounded by green vegetation, the aspect is one of brilliant color. Any somber lava blacks are overwhelmed by the blues of sky and sea and by the luxuriant greenery.

The site itself was largely barren lava during the height of its occupancy, with only some shady groves of trees along the coast. When explorers and merchants arrived, inadvertently carrying seeds of thorny shrubs and other foreign vegetation, they introduced an exotic flora that is currently being removed in order to restore the integrity of the historic site. Native plants, such as pandanus, kou, and pili (a source of thatch for grass houses), are being kept or reestablished.

A visitor, on arrival, stands amid coconut palms and looks across the sand and dark-rock shores toward the sea. Out there are tidal pools that abound with fish, and the visitor may watch Hawaiian men or women perched on the black shore boulders trying their luck with rod and line or throw net.

Coconut palms stand in and around the ruins as if trying to fix them in place and stabilize them. The gray trunks, horizontally ribbed, are often intricately designed and roughened, as though some ancient god had tried to scratch his initials in some strange script. Very few of these trunks, which form almost a stockade wall when crowded, are straight. They lean and curve, and we expect to hear a crashing sound at any time, as one goes down. Their fronds overhead are thinly lacerated leaves, which form a complex, interlocking pattern, the kind of design that might result if bright green combs were hooked together at random.

The monkeypod tree stands as a stalwart off to one side. Pandanus trees, which are not as tall or as graceful as the monkeypod, have a bushier foliage and their trunks have forms that could illustrate the principles of advanced geometry. But life at the Place of Refuge is influenced most by the coconut, a tree whose shade we find most welcome before we venture out onto the open volcanic rock.

The lava on which the visitor walks is made of curving designs, the result of rolling flows that came to a stop before plunging into the sea. The lava shelf is generally horizontal, its surface composed of rounded plates and shallow troughs, small hummocks, and twisted flows. In a few low places water remains in scattered puddles whose surfaces are utterly still, reflecting the white and blue of the Pacific sky.

It is tempting to wander for hours along this shore, but the thought of man's mysterious goings-on keeps coming back like a ghost from the deep. A place of refuge? Why here? Why at all?

The idea of havens and sanctuaries is, of course, widespread and timeless. There have been refuges for the soul, for animal life, for artifacts, and so on, perhaps even before the beginning of recorded history. Numbers 35, in the Old Testament of the Christian Bible, tells how God spoke to Moses on the plains of Moab near Jericho:

> And among the cities which ye shall give unto the Levites there shall be six cities for refuge, which ye shall appoint for the man-slayer, that he may flee thither . . . .
>
> And the congregation shall deliver the slayer out of the hand of the revenger of blood, and the congregation shall restore him to the city of his refuge, whither he was fled: and he shall abide in it unto the death of the high priest, which was anointed with the holy oil.
>
> But if the slayer shall at any time come without the border of the city of his refuge, whither he was fled;
>
> And the revenger of blood find him without the borders of the city of his refuge, and the revenger of blood kill the slayer; he shall not be guilty of blood:
>
> Because he should have remained in the city of his refuge until the death of the high priest: but after the death of the high priest the slayer shall return into the land of his possession.

But at this Hawaiian site the concept was enlarged to a highly sophisticated degree by an early Pacific culture, and the parallel is extraordinary.

Here was a spot of land—little more than that, less than 20 acres in all—where any man, woman, child, friend, or enemy could escape the rigors of a society from which it seemed expedient to flee.

Variously, this notion manifests itself today in forms with which we are

City of Refuge
National Historical Park, Hawaii:
far left–restored temple of Hale-o-Keawe;
left–idols near temple;
bottom–great wall at Place of Refuge

more familiar, but in the society of ancient Hawaii the rules were considerably different. Perhaps what strikes us most is the establishment, then and now, of places where men could obtain relief from the world. And it looks as though the Hawaiian Place of Refuge was more secure than any available today.

Given the severity of ancient Hawaiian conflicts, it is rather hard to understand the peaceful influence of a simple temple, or heiau (pronounced *hay-ah-oo*). The early Hawaiians took wars for granted, planned them, prepared for them, started them, and put every energy into them. War was a matter of total extermination of the enemy.

But whoever managed to reach these grounds was admitted and could neither be punished nor apprehended within. That rule was sacred. Each refugee stayed as long as he thought he had to, and when the battle from which he fled was over he returned to his home in peace. Most refugees stayed only overnight, or a few days at most.

Such an arrangement granted to the prevailing religious system a power apparently greater than that of any military or judicial system among those Hawaiians. From man's contemporary experience it may seem too much to expect that a simple temple could shelter fleeing combatants or noncombatants in the heat of battle.

Perhaps that was the reason for the great wall. In the social thinking of other societies, past and present, it has seemed to make good sense to erect some kind of wall—high, thick, or long—to restrict the passage of human beings. If such were the case at the Place of Refuge, then the great black wall that confronts us has a meaning more readily understood: defense.

The wall emerges from the palms and crosses the lava parallel to shore for a distance of more than 600 feet, then turns and heads toward the sea for another 400 feet. As it averages 10 feet in height one is not able to scale it easily. Its thickness is not a mere 6 feet or so, which would have kept out battering rams (if such there were), but 17 feet.

This is a tantalizing mystery. Why so wide? With the lack of written records, we cannot tell. Yet the wall itself is a record of sorts. The black lava blocks were laid without mortar, which was easy enough to accomplish, considering the roughness of the stone; but some blocks, measuring nearly seven feet high, must weigh close to five tons. They were hefted into place by a people who had no metals or wheels. They did, however, have levers of hard wood, such as ohia and kauila.

To deepen the mystery, there are hollows within the wall, which modern legend says were secret passageways. Actually, archaeological examination has revealed that the hollows, too small to hold a man, were probably a technique of construction intended to conserve rock; no continuous passageways existed.

In 1779, Capt. James Cook was killed by Hawaiians on the shore of Kealakekua Bay, four miles to the north of here, where a monument to him has been erected. With all his troubles, Cook had insufficient time to explore and describe the vicinity; his men did leave a fragmentary but accurate account of the Hale-o-Keawe, a temple that was in use between about 1650 and 1819 and is now restored.

The earliest detailed picture of the Place of Refuge was given by the Reverend William Ellis, an early missionary. He visited the site in 1823 and wrote:

> The principal object that attracted our attention, was the [Hale-o-Keawe], a sacred depository of the bones of departed kings and princes, probably erected for the reception of the bones of the king whose name it bears, and who reigned in Hawaii about eight generations back.
>
> It is a compact building, twenty-four feet by sixteen, constructed with the most durable timber, and thatched with ti leaves, standing on a bed of lava that runs out a considerable distance into the sea. . . .
>
> Several rudely carved male and female images of wood were placed on the outside of the enclosure; some on low pedestals under the shade of an adjacent tree, others on high posts on the jutting rocks that hung over the edge of the water.
>
> A number stood on the fence at unequal distances all around; but the principal assemblage of these frightful representatives of their former deities was at the south-east end of the enclosed space, where, forming a semicircle, twelve of them stood in grim array, as if per-

petual guardians of "the mighty dead" reposing in the house adjoin-ing. . . .

Once they had evidently been clothed, but now they appeared in the most indigent nakedness. A few tattered shreds round the neck of one that stood on the left hand side of the door, rotted by the rain and bleached by the sun, were all that remained of numerous and gaudy garments, with which their votaries had formerly arrayed them. . . .

We endeavoured to gain admission to the inside of the house, but were told . . . that nothing but a direct order from the king . . . could open the door.

However, by pushing one of the boards across the door-way a little on one side, we looked in, and saw many large images, some of wood very much carved, others of red feathers, with distended mouths, large rows of sharks' teeth, and pearl-shell eyes.

We also saw several bundles, apparently of human bones, cleaned, carefully tied up . . . and placed in different parts of the house, to-gether with some rich shawls and other valuable articles, probably worn by those to whom the bones belonged, as the wearing ap-parel and other personal property of the chiefs is generally buried with them. . . .

[The Place of Refuge] afforded an inviolable sanctuary to the guilty fugitive, who, when flying from the avenging spear, was so favoured as to enter their precincts. . . .

To whomsoever he belonged, and from whatever part he came, he was equally certain of admittance, though liable to be pursued even to the gates of the enclosure.

Happily for him, those gates were perpetually open; and as soon as the fugitive had entered, he repaired to the presence of the idol, and made a short ejaculatory address, expressive of his obligations to him in reaching the place with security.

At times there may have been hundreds of people within the walls, especially if wars were raging outside. Mark Twain, who visited the site in 1866, gave his imagination free rein:

> *In those days, if a man killed another anywhere on the Island the relatives were privileged to take the murderer's life; and then a chase for life and liberty began—the outlawed criminal flying through path-less forests and over mountain and plain, with his hopes fixed upon the protecting walls of the City of Refuge, and the avenger of blood following hotly after him! Sometimes the race was kept up to the very gates of the temple, and the panting pair sped through long files of excited natives, who watched the contest with flashing eye and dilated nostril, encouraging the hunted refugee with sharp, inspiriting ejaculations, and sending up a ringing shout of exultation when the saving gates closed upon him and the cheated pursuer sank exhausted at the threshold. But sometimes the flying criminal fell under the hand of the avenger at the very door, when one more brave stride, one more brief second of time would have brought his feet upon the sacred ground and barred him against all harm.*

Most likely this is an overdramatization of events that actually occurred, but there can be little doubt that great drama was played out here.

King Kamehameha I ruled from this place. In fact, one finds in the vicinity the graves of his warriors and foes who fell in the 1782 battle of Mokuohai, which started consolidation of Kamehameha's power over the island of Hawaii.

There are several temple structures in and near the walls of the Place of Refuge, as well as dwelling sites, stone idols, pens for keeping domestic animals taken in tax collections, ceremonial stones, pavement, fishponds that were once Kamehameha's, burial caves, and old canoe landings. There were also trails and paths made of smooth-sided lava blocks or of rounded stones from the shore of the sea, causeways, ramps, and royal sledding tracks hundreds of feet long.

These last were inclined slopes overlain with rocks and covered with earth and dry grass to make them slippery; competitive sledding on them was a sport for kings—and only kings.

After the death of Kamehameha I in 1819, the practice of idolatry was abolished, but the Place of Refuge remained sacrosanct in the minds of the people for many years after. Here were housed the bones of Hawaiian royalty until 1829, and on these grounds was the mausoleum for the Kamehameha family.

Eventually the site was abandoned. The wooden figures decayed and fell, or were taken away. High waves battered the site but could not dislodge the stones. Nor could they wash away the spirit of the Place of Refuge or drown the memories of what had happened there.

In the late 1800s the property was acquired by the Bishop Estate. Repairs and restorations commenced early in the twentieth century. The site was leased to the County of Hawaii as a park, and finally, after authorization by an act of Congress in 1955, established as the City of Refuge National Historical Park. The park's stated purpose, then and henceforth, was for the benefit and inspiration of the people.

Yet aside from enjoyment, and despite the shadowed mysteries, a brief visit to the Place of Refuge and a sojourn among the Hawaiians leave us with thoughts we might not have had before . . .

. . . that language, and in this case the lilting, lovely flow of Hawaiian words, unveils a great deal about the senses and sensibilities of a people. . . .

. . . that what men think of disrespectfully as paganism possesses worthy attributes, and that peoples who practiced it belonged to a culture adapted to their surroundings. They had time to think, to dream, to love, to work, to worship, which is about the maximum that any human culture can ask of life.

Reverend Ellis himself said that here idolatry appeared at least in a form of clemency. Perhaps the site was established, he said, by ancient priests. Or by some humane prince who wished to reduce the cruelties of their customs or soften the anguish of savage warfare. Or through some connection with the cities of refuge of the Israelites.

Here, too, we find that modern men with vision recognized this hallowed point of land as a significant representation of the original Hawaii and had the maturity to set it aside for the benefit of all Americans and the citizens of the world.

We wander in peace and solitude beneath the coconut palms, beyond the great black wall, and past the remains of the wide heiaus to the sea.

As we watch the waters wash the lava shelf, swirl for a while, and then return, we think of that vanished race of men—Kamehameha, his warriors, his enemies, his descendants—who rose for a time, lived out their lives on these islands, and fell. As other men on other islands fell.

The whole Pacific pulses here. In this little point of land lies not only the heart of Hawaiian history but also the epitome of cultures and beliefs and beauty that are as wide as this widest of oceans.

The cultures of the early Pacific peoples are worlds apart from the cultures of a number of countries today. The little we have of their history suggests that they were noble. Their descendants were and are noble, as one can readily see in the Maoris, the Tahitians, the Samoans, and the Hawaiians themselves.

The Place of Refuge is a tangible vestige of the past, a place of silence and peace. It is almost as if a play has ended and the characters have made their exit, never to return. But we still have a portion of the stage, and, with the gift of our imagination, that is all we need.

For long moments we watch the sea. The white salt waves surge up and over the lava, into the teeming tidal pools, and back again to the coral shallows or down to the darker depths.

It is then that we realize how men and their energies come and go as waves at the edge of the sea—all temporary. But like the seas themselves, here and perhaps elsewhere in the universe, the fundamental currents of life go on, as far as we know, forever.

Verde Valley, Arizona 🐛

A NARROW SHAFT OF SUNSHINE PIERCED THE CANOPY OF cottonwood and willow, spotlighted the petals of a yellow columbine, and caused them to glow like a candle suddenly lighted in the shadows.

A soft breeze, redolent with the fresh aroma of new spring growth, touched the flower and turned it into a flickering golden beacon. Immediately a humming-bird came into view, stopped in midair, maneuvered to the columbine and probed for a moment, then swept away as quickly as it had come.

No sooner had it gone than a yellow warbler suddenly sang in the syca-more overhead. Its high-pitched notes sounded almost hollow in the little dell; they trailed away in delicate tones, their echoes sprinkling like falling water from a mossy seep.

The density of the vegetation made us feel a little like explorers pene-trating the Panamanian jungle rather than patrolling a desert stream in Arizona. We crept as silently as possible, or hopped from rock to rock to avoid a rus-tling of leaves and consequent disturbance of the natural community. Unques-tionably, we saw and heard far more this way than we would have by plowing brutishly through the brush.

The rapids of Beaver Creek, beyond the fringing shrubs, glittered with tiny suns turning on and off as the waters caught and lost them in reflection.

Above the rapids and eddy pools, insects darted while a waiting black phoebe sat on a seepwillow branch and watched. Away from the water a blue grosbeak sang, probably near a wild grape tangle, and its song filled the vale with robinlike notes.

Along the edge of the stream spread a lattice of interlaced sycamore limbs, their bark a mottled brown and white. Some limbs reached out over the water and dipped down toward it, resembling a row of pale giraffes about to drink.

Not far away, a cream-colored limestone cliff bordered the creek for a hundred yards at a point where the creek had in centuries past sliced off the side of a low white hill. The sycamores towered 30 or 40 feet up the side of the cliff, then launched their limbs out over the arid land on top.

What a contrast! Up there, away from the humid stream environment, grew thorny catclaws and mesquites, copses of creosote bush, and low-level herbs like snakeweed. Lizards scampered from one patch of shadow to another, paying no mind, apparently, to the flow of treble notes from a black-throated sparrow in a barberry bush.

The change was stark. Up over the face of the cliff we had come to find a milieu as dry as the creek was wet. A different way of life existed out in the open—no columbines, no phoebes, no sycamores, no water. Down there along the stream, as at a desert oasis, nearly everything depended on water, whereas life up here in a land with less than ten inches of rain per year, was a balanced collection of organisms independent of streams.

That two such habitats could coexist so closely would seem little short of amazing to a newcomer. But he would hardly have time to wonder about it because of another surprise in store. For this was a special hill.

From the top of it, a few steps farther on, we came to the brink of a wide open pit, a natural limestone sink, more than 500 feet across, with a pond below and towering cottonwoods within.

This different environment of marsh and pond possessed still another set of residents: coots pattering over the surface, uttering squawks and shrieks; turtles at rest on fallen logs; muskrats making their way in winding trails through the floating banks of pondweed.

Within the sink at our feet were caves. On the distant rim of the valley spread a forest of pines decorated with mountain bluebells and Steller jays. Each ecosystem was endowed with its own specific music and musicians and its own *dramatis animalia*.

In what others might regard as a dreary desert landscape, the naturalist and the artist and the philosopher—professional or otherwise—could find here a paradise to challenge their fondest dreams.

For two years we lived in the Verde Valley of central Arizona, a place both desert and mountain, canyon and prairie, cold and hot, wet and dry. We often thought it had everything, and that everything happened at once.

The outpost where we lived, Montezuma Well, a detached portion of Montezuma Castle National Monument, was fairly isolated then, and many a visitor asked: "Whatever do you do out here, all by yourself?"

It became increasingly difficult to suppress a smile on answering that perfectly honest and serious question. Our usual reply was: "We try to get caught up on all the things we want to do!"

But we never got caught up. The Verde Valley, 15 miles wide by 30 miles long, possesses a rare concentration of secrets. Some are quite obvious. Oak Creek Canyon, at the northern side of the valley, is conspicuous and magnificent, and U.S. Highway 89 is regarded by some as the most beautiful drive in North America.

The northern end of the Verde Valley possesses formations similar to those in the upper walls of the Grand Canyon, and therefore has its share of color: white limestone rims, cream-colored sandstone cliffs, and blood red terraces of shale. Blended with all this is a fascinating flora and fauna that in these pages we lack the space even to introduce. A lifetime in and around Oak Creek Canyon produces the feeling that other lifetimes are necessary to understand it.

But elsewhere, as you look out over the valley of the Rio Verde, there seems to be little more than farmland, low white limestone hills that gleam too brightly in a heat too often intense, and flats of creosote bush that look as though they had not had water in years and could not shelter much in the way of animal life.

The valley is a product of the Verde River, an idyllic desert stream lined with cottonwoods, sycamores, and grassed and flowered banks. The place where we

Montezuma Castle National Monument, Arizona:
top–Montezuma Castle;
left–yellow columbine;
bottom–portals to the Verde Valley

lived, Montezuma Well, lay on Beaver Creek, a tributary of the Verde River that is equally luxuriant with vegetation.

The white limestone of the Verde Valley, laid down in an ancient lake, has been dissolved by water into underground networks of channels and passageways and is pocked with caves. From the sandstone and lava plateaus to the north and west, where heavy rain and snow fall at high elevations, water sinks into the porous surface and percolates down to the valley, reaches an impermeable stratum of rock, then works along this surface until it pours out at some point in the Verde limestone.

There it emerges as springs and artesian wells. Only rarely have water-filled caves been near enough to the surface to have fallen in and become natural limestone sinks. The best example in the valley, and perhaps in the West, is Montezuma Well, named after the Aztec chieftain who never saw it. The well receives water from some subterranean source, and the pond within it remains a constant 470 feet across and 55 feet in depth.

On coming to the rim of the well for the first time, one may be forgiven for thinking of it as an ancient Mayan *cenote* into which maidens and children were flung as sacrifice to the gods. The resemblance is superficial, since such a practice, as far as is known, did not take place here. Indians inhabited the rim and the walls of the well, and the ruins of their pueblo structures as well as their cliff dwellings may be seen.

Indians have occupied the Verde Valley for 4,000 years or so, but not until about A.D. 600 did they establish much more than temporary campsites. The first permanent settlers, now called Hohokam, came from the south and built pit houses of poles, brush, and mud. One has been unearthed, protected, and displayed at Montezuma Well, although only the configurations of the floor remain to tell us that the dwelling had wall posts, a fire pit, an entry way, and a draft deflector. As such pit houses go, it was rather large by comparison with others and may have been a gathering place for religious ceremonies and meetings.

The social functions of the Hohokam, and the Sinagua groups who came into the valley later, are obscured by the absence of written records. But the use these cultures made of the region is very clear indeed. They farmed small plots of corn, beans, squash, and cotton, irrigating them with water diverted from the outlet of Montezuma Well—a steady supply of a thousand gallons a minute.

Having filtered through so much limestone, the water absorbed a high content of calcium carbonate. This precipitated out and lined the ancient canals with lime, just as hard water leaves a coating of lime on the inner surfaces of modern teakettles.

The dust and soil of centuries have long since filled and buried the Indian canals, some of which were over a mile in length. The debris has been scooped out of one small section, however, and one can see the limestone lining of the walls.

The water from Montezuma Well issues dependably all year, and probably always has. The modern canal that carried it split above our house and flowed on both sides. Day and night, therefore, we heard the music of gently falling water, as though tiny bells were drifting beneath the windows.

On nearly any day of the year at least 30 species of birds sang around the house or within hearing distance, and their songs were a special source of interest. Some birds came for the winter, such as flocks of white-crowned sparrows; a few, like the Lewis woodpecker, ventured down only when the mountains were covered with heavy snow.

The mild winter climate of the Verde Valley (a temperature range of 9 to 60 degrees in one day is not unusual) yields early to the coming of spring. The first plant flowers in January, an event unknown to all but a few human beings. If we sought the secret places in which it grew—facing the sun, protected a bit from the wintry winds that sometimes cooled the Verde flats—then we would be rewarded with the tiny purple blossoms of *Cymopterus multinervatus*. We knew no other name for it. As a member of the parsnip family it had familiar complex leaves. Most people never went hunting for it, and quite possibly while it bloomed they were still shivering and hoping that a sign of spring would come.

Yet there it was, inconspicuous, defenseless, uncommon—though tended with the same kind of care that the forces of creation and sustenance and evolution give to a galaxy.

We searched for it each January, or perhaps in February if the winter was late. We watched for the play of its colorful corollas, the thickening of stems and leaves. We saw it burst open on a patch of blank ground, and were grateful each time for a gift that so gladdened our hearts.

It was the first of many gifts. The circle of seasons called forth an extraordinary treasure of flowers, from delicate wild orchids to the dry-land creosote bush. No walk, no patrol, no research was ever routine. We scouted, discovered, puzzled, pieced together clues, and collected notes for follow-up quests. The barberry, for example, presented a handsome show of yellow flowers, but we made a point of returning for the later profusion of brilliant orange berries.

The region around the well was a veritable garden. Without much trouble one could find anemone, buttercup, delphinium, buckwheat, phlox, aster, and cardinal flower. Scores of species bloomed at once in spring, and during most of the year a little searching could reveal at least a few flowers in bloom.

Many managed to survive out where the sun baked the dry but well-vegetated flats. The little filaree, a member of the geranium family and introduced into the Southwest perhaps by early Spaniards, sometimes carpeted the open spots in brilliant magenta.

Big bushy bouquets of four-o'clock came out even in the driest of dry spells. This was a heartening sight, representative of the long millenniums of evolutionary adaptation to little rain. These flowers may receive the proper amount of moisture months before, which permits their surging forth in the searing summer heat, and therefore reproducing regardless of drought.

There is much being learned about the physiological functions of desert plants, and man will no doubt learn some day how patterns of growth relate to the master rhythms of the universe. In our own lifetime we are unlikely to learn the answers to riddles presented by even the simplest species; but each of us, in his own secret places, is free to wonder and try to seek the answers.

In summer the thunderheads sometimes built up directly overhead, filling the deep blue Arizona sky with roiling mists of black and gray. Once while we were gone, lightning followed a telephone line from a bluff nearby, blew open the telephone in the kitchen, ripped up the sink and counter, and blasted the outside phone box 30 feet away.

There were moments of intense color when sunsets tinged the sky with gold and orange and red. On such summer evenings, vermilion flycatchers often flew up into the air and uttered their glorious songs, which had the effect of slender, tuneful crystals striking each other at the touch of the wind. No chamber music could have been more harmonious.

On rare occasions a roadrunner rattled its notes from some still perch in a mesquite tree on the cliff above. This soliloquy did not last very long, however; a few moments later the bird would unfold its wings and swoop in a gentle glide down to the flats of creosote bush where it would sweep out of view.

We witnessed such sights and sounds primarily when remaining completely motionless, eyes observing, ears alert, senses tuned to the frequencies of the wild. It therefore occurred to us that if we devoted one day almost entirely to "doing nothing," we would be likely to see things that our eyes did not normally reveal to us.

The idea was hardly new, of course, but it was novel to us at the time. We had admired Thoreau's independence in this regard, yet simply had never gotten down to doing anything of the sort ourselves. There did not seem to be much need for it because we were surrounded by wildlife as it was.

And besides, with so much to do, so much to get caught up on, so many places to go—no, this time we would get up, eat, set out, and sit—sit all day if we wanted to.

We would try to get over to Beaver Creek if events warranted, but only if and when we pleased or nature dictated. We would watch a sycamore tree, or a butterfly on a milkweed, or listen to the cuckoo in the cottonwood. We would stay. Nothing would compel us to leave before we had finished following whatever we were after. We might even lie on a rock in the sun and, of all things, have a short nap.

By quite a good many people, this would be regarded as a thoroughly wasted day. We would be branded as loafers, condemned to perdition for failing the Lord's work, and chastised for not giving each waking hour to personal advancement and human achievement. For a while we had a few doubts.

What brought us around was watching a man one day walk up to the rim of Montezuma Well and stop in his tracks about 20 steps before reaching the edge. Since he could not see the depression from there, something else must have distracted him. We followed his gaze to a twisted juniper tree growing back from the rim. It was a tree that thousands of persons scarcely noticed as they passed by in their eagerness to get to the well.

His eyes roved up and down the tree, and for a long time he stood without moving. To be sure, it was an interesting tree. It was gnarled and twisted, as most junipers are, and its bark shone golden reddish brown in the afternoon sunlight. Its limbs were thrust in various attitudes, like an Oriental dancer who seemed to have both arms and legs in motion at once.

Patches of leaves were placed at just the right locations, so when one looked at the tree long enough, it took on the appearance of having been fashioned with grace and skill.

The more he looked at the tree, the more the man obviously became captivated. Soon there was no other world around him; he and the tree appeared to have formed some sort of cosmic bond.

He motioned his friends to go on. They nodded with understanding, as if to say, "Well, there he goes again," and left.

After a while he sat on a limestone block and for nearly an hour studied the tree. Only now and then did his eyes move up to the sky and the clouds, or to the cactus and creosote bush around him, or to the blue mountains in the distance. These were brief interruptions. His eyes always came quickly back to the juniper.

That did it. If he could find so much enjoyment in a simple thing, others also could.

Therefore we decided to take a whole day to find our own trees, and perhaps hear something of the message the man at the well had seemed to hear.

For one glorious day we let everything go, forgot the schedules, forgot the routine tasks, forgot the clock, forgot the critics, forgot everything except the sycamores and cottonwoods, the cuckoos and roadrunners. And for the first time we would follow them wherever *they* went, not merely hope to see them wherever *we* went.

The day brimmed over with surprises. Not all of them are easy to remember because so many new experiences crowded in for attention that we could only remember the highlights.

We separated from ourselves, went through a space-time barrier, and became engulfed with greenery, with music, with warmth from the sun, with solitude, with our own inquisitive spell of wonder.

There is nothing fancied about this. We had sampled it in bits and pieces before. Most people, at one time or another, experience such exhilaration. It was simply the reaction of human beings in natural release, free to think, free to wander, free to be happy and cheerful, free to hear and be humble.

A handsome song came out of the sycamore trees. Two tanagers, she a dull yellow and he as red as a cardinal flower, flew past a wild grape tangle and into a cluster of cottonwoods. We followed as far as we could, observing their diligent search for insects, wondering whether their lives might well be as complex as those of men.

And if the male tanagers had become so brightly colored through the adaptations of evolution, why had not the males in all other species as well?

There was no time to muse, for another mystery suddenly confronted us.

A short time before, we had heard the house finch's song, an extremely complex rendition, but always the same. Over and over—how many hundreds of times in a day?—its song was delivered with little variation.

Now from the woods came an entirely different sound—a chatter, like two birds talking to one another.

Twelve rapid raucous notes, 2 beeps, 5 screeches, a gulp, 11 raucous notes, 4 beeps, 11 notes again, a squawk, 3 peeps, a gulp, 4 beeps, 13 notes, and so on.

It was the long-tailed chat—no victim of conformity! We had heard it often, occasionally at night, and sometimes all night. But not until now had we wondered why the chat had come to be endowed with multiple voices whereas the finch was destined to sing one song forever.

Gila woodpeckers kept us company almost constantly. Rarely silent, often flying from tree to tree in the bottomlands, their hammering could frequently be heard, and the sound rattled the forest.

How pleasant it was to wander through the woods and across the fields, not caring what time it was, or how much "success" we had achieved so far. Which way we walked was not important because we were not going anywhere. We were cast out, cut off, marooned, and stranded—and savoring every free and precious minute of it.

We followed old trails along stream terraces, where ant lions made their holes. We saw tracks of deer in the soft sands, breathed in the sweet damp air that swayed the branches gently and rustled sharp-pointed sycamore leaves.

The high-spirited arguments of ash-throated flycatchers filled us with a cheer that was to last for years.

At the edge of Beaver Creek we came to a long, quiet pool that lay hidden beneath the willows. The lacework of leaves arching over it formed a tunnel, green and cool and insulated from all but the sounds of birds. At the upper end of the pool we got out some old air mattresses reserved there for floating on the pond, settled on them, and pushed away from shore.

It took almost an hour to drift from one end of the pool to the other, time enough to observe the streamside community in detail. We were not intruders, but quiet, watchful visitors of minimum visibility within this environment, flooded with the delicate aroma of the streamside, of moisture, decay, new growth, of alders, willows, and fresh flowers.

We knew that muskrats and beavers inhabited the banks and terraces upstream or down, but for the most part they were quiet at midday. So were mice, rats, rabbits, and raccoons that lived along the banks.

Such an oasis in so wide a desert is bound to have a large population of water-loving organisms. Birds patrolled the ribbon of green and we could hear the call of the kingfisher as it flew erratically from one perch to another along the bank.

From the shade and canopy that kept out the harsh sun's rays of midday, fell the music of various songbirds. We found ourselves differentiating between the notes of warblers—yellow and Lucy's particularly—and thinking of the words of William H. Hudson in *Green Mansions*:

"And caring not in that solitude to disguise my feelings from myself, and from the wide heaven that looked down and saw me—for this is the sweetest thing that solitude has for us, that we are free in it, and no convention holds us—I dropped on my knees and kissed the stony ground, then casting up my eyes, thanked the Author of my being for the gift of that wild forest, those green mansions where I had found so great a happiness!"

What else happened that afternoon is lost in the forgetfulness of time, or was so completely of another world as to lie beyond the space-time barrier.

We came home more refreshed than ever before, more rested, more full of the adventures that had turned our minds around. Adventures, illusions, thoughts, images—a whole year's supply!

Of course, our trousers were torn by the gripping thorns of catclaw. We had stumbled over fallen cottonwood limbs while looking up instead of down. Our feet got caught among the lava boulders that lay strewn over the floodplain. We got sunburned and windburned and tired and a little sore.

But we had gotten our first close look at a hackberry leaf—an extraordinary network of veins. We had seen a globemallow flower, delicate orange, nestled in the curving arc of a dead and de-barked cottonwood limb—which itself had been artfully engraved by beetles. These sights—the hackberry leaf, the sculptured limb, the fragile flower—paid for every pain and peril.

The day taught us how to enjoy more fully other aspects of the Verde Valley. We went to the rim of Montezuma Well each morning, creeping up silently and unobtrusively, and in this way saw dozens of species of waterfowl.

One morning we watched a mother raccoon bring four young ones down to the water's edge for a drink. Another time, while walking the edge of a bluff, we stopped in our tracks and looked down into the eyes of a fox less than ten feet away. Remaining motionless we piqued the animal's curiosity. It did not know what to do. It had barely noticed any movement. It could see our outlines, and perhaps felt the need to flee. But it had to know, and to know it must stay, remaining motionless, too. Thus vis-à-vis we stood for perhaps five minutes, two species of animals, each looking into the other's eyes, linked for a few minutes, facing each other in some sort of harmony about which neither knew much, if anything.

Away from the well were hundreds of things to do and discover. The bright white limestone of the Verde Valley had been deposited in an ancient lake that backed up like a reservoir when volcanic eruptions near Squaw Peak, at the valley's southern end, poured out and blocked the ancestral Verde River.

Leopards, camels, and mammoths occupied the shores of the lake during deposition of the Verde limestone, and today one finds the footprints of those creatures converted into solid rock. We came upon tracks so large they seemed like craters, but were obviously made by a heavy-bodied mammal, such as a mammoth, which trudged in the shallows or through the mud. Intermixed were tracks that looked like those of a tiger, but we could only speculate.

In time, the lava dam was worn away; the Verde River and its tributaries eroded downward, into limestone and beds of boulders and conglomerate, into unconsolidated muds, and finally into thick deposits of salt that had resulted from repeated evaporation of saline waters in an arid climate.

The salt beds lie near the little village of Camp Verde, and gleam like an enormous mound of snow and ice. Contained in the beds is sodium sulfate in several forms—glauberite, thenardite, mirabilite—but most abundant is sodium chloride, the common halite of table salt.

We spent many an hour poking around where prehistoric Indians had been the first to work. They tunneled in and down for perhaps a hundred feet, but failed to shore up the ceilings; these collapsed at times and buried them alive. Human remains have been exhumed from the old salt tunnels, as well as a quantity of crude stone axes, blunt and better suited to chopping skulls than salt. But the Indians got what they wanted; salt was valuable to them.

In more recent times the salts were mined commercially—trucked out, crushed, washed, sprayed, dissolved, dried, screened, and shaken. But these operations did not last very long and the diggings are now defunct.

We were never idle; after all, the Verde limestone covered 300 square miles. Many eroded pockets within it contained the remains of prehistoric cliff dwellings. And Tuzigoot, a hilltop Indian dwelling, was a veritable fortress of more than a hundred rooms.

If we wanted the flavor of the old frontier, there was always Jerome, a ghost town clinging to the cliffs and slopes on the western wall of the valley.

Rocks in that area are chiefly slate and diorite shot through with light-colored granites and pegmatites. They have been folded, crushed, and metamorphosed, and if anything in the history of mountains ever pointed to the formation of valuable minerals, this was it. The twisted, distorted, turned-up-on-end formations are prominent at the portals to the valley near Jerome.

Along the Verde fault, where crustal movement has been taking place since Precambrian time, minerals were deposited in pockets, cracks, and vugs.

To look at the mountains today, and at Jerome crumbling into ruin, it is hard to believe that once you could hear the rattle of ore trains, echoes of smelter whistles, and the grinding and grating of a major mining complex.

In 1876 a pioneer farmer discovered ore and staked two claims, the Eureka and Wade Hampton. Copper showed in abundance but interest was not particularly high because the nearest railroad terminal was at Las Animas, Colorado.

By 1882, the Santa Fe, then known as the Atlantic & Pacific, had laid down rails across northern Arizona, and that made transportation of ores in this region seem economically feasible. Influential Arizonans enlisted financial aid, including that of Eugene Jerome of New York City, after whom the growing town was named, and set to work. They failed in two years, primarily for having to haul the ore by mule team over approximately 60 miles of wagon road to the rails at Ash Fork.

But in an era of opening ore fields in the West, these mines were soon connected with the outside world by a narrow-gage railroad. By 1910 production was booming, a smelter site had been located on the Verde River, and eventually two more railroads were constructed to or within the valley.

The Jerome Mining District, a complex network of faults, covered a strip of steep terrain along the flank of the mountain. The main orebody, a lens-shaped shaft, or pipe, with a cross-sectional area of about 12 acres, outcropped above Jerome and plunged under the town for how deeply no one knew.

It was surrounded by quartz and diorite, which were very durable and had to be removed. So hard was the rock that drilling holes for explosives required a substantial quantity of steel. Most drills were about an inch in diameter and the sharpening shop handled around 2,000 pieces daily.

All blasting was done by electrical means, which meant that stray currents could be dangerous. Since the rock did not offer a positive ground everywhere, an elaborate system of wires sunk in subterranean creek bottoms and strung throughout the mine had to be installed, and everything creating electrical currents was connected to it.

When the miners finally reached pay dirt, scarcely one-seventh of the volume of ore was worth taking out. In spite of these handicaps, however, the United Verde grew into a major mining concern and produced nearly 2 million tons of ore in its peak year (1929).

Many types of minerals existed, including silver, lead, zinc, and iron, but copper was king, and the most important ore was a copper sulfide, chalcopyrite. It was also a hazard.

Like other sulfides, chalcopyrite gave off a highly flammable gas and the slightest spark was enough to set it off. Thus in 1894 the mine "blew up"; several upper levels caught fire and had to be sealed off. Some levels burned for years, making entry into and mining of them impossible.

Even surface operations were hampered. Since the fires sealed some sections of the mine, the logical solution was open-pit operation. This commenced in 1918 and it took the first nine years merely to strip away 8 million cubic yards of surface material. Hot ground was encountered, and when the miners went deeper the heat from adjacent burning chambers became unbearable.

Holes drilled for blasting sometimes reached a temperature of 780 degrees. Workers cooled the holes with water or sand before dropping the dynamite in, or else "torpedoed" the holes, a process by which explosives were insulated, lowered into the hole by a piece of wire, and detonated.

After being extracted, the ore was carried in 90-ton capacity cars down the Verde Tunnel and Smelter Railroad, unloaded at the crushing plant, sorted, and reduced to bits less than one-fourth of an inch in diameter. Crushed ore went to the roaster plant, where it was subjected to temperatures high enough to remove impurities, then into the reverberators. These were brick kilns, measuring 25 by 100 feet, where the ore was melted and the slag skimmed off. The result was copper matte, a mixture of copper and iron sulfides about 35 percent pure copper.

Matte was then poured into the converter, or final stage, blown through with air to oxidize and take out the iron, skimmed of slag, blown again and again to blister copper, and poured into bars. Because it was a shade less than pure it had to be shipped to refineries elsewhere.

All this smelting produced dense clouds of smoke that hung like a pall over the valley. In 1918 a smoke-treating plant was designed and constructed, perhaps as much to assuage complaining farmers as to recover 11,000 pounds of copper escaping daily as dust and gases from the various plants.

During the peak year, converters turned out 12 million pounds of bullion a month. But this was not to last. For the United Verde, as for other companies mining in the valley, time ran out.

Closing down in the Depression years only delayed the end. In 1940, open-pit operations ceased and by 1948 the mine had run out of ore. The smelter closed two years later, and at last the "Big Hole" was dead. It had produced $475 million worth of ore.

Thus went the mining era from the Verde Valley—the rattling ore trains, the clanks and grinds and whistles and smoke. The old open-pit remains abandoned and silent. The fires below are dead. Jerome still clings with tenacity to the slope, which is slowly coming apart. The houses crumble. The jail has slid, and still slides, down the mountain.

But Jerome's inhabitants take pride in their town and its historic role in western mining. They preserve as much of its character as they can in museums, exhibits, booklets—and the tales of old-timers who were there in the heyday and can tell you a thing or two about the poker games that used to go on in the saloons. . . .

*　　*　　*

From every trip in the Verde Valley we came home exuberant with a new supply of discoveries—so close, so familiar, yet virtually unknown before.

Each time it was like launching a new adventure, toward an untold number of secrets, all waiting to be revealed. And the only requirements had been curiosity, receptivity, open eyes, and open ears.

We captured on tape the music of the western meadowlark, and now can hear it at any time, reclaiming a few of the magic moments that thrilled us then.

We photographed, painted, sketched, looked, listened, studied. We sat on promontories and made time-lapse motion pictures of clouds in the sky. We fed the white-crowned sparrows in winter, and waked to the drumming of the Gila woodpecker.

Coming in exhausted after each expedition was all a part of the pleasure and the experience. How we slept with the song of falling water outside!

Coming back on duty after such explorations—near or far—the first activity was to see what ducks had come to the well since the day before. We crept up silently and, of course, never passed the juniper tree without remembering the man who had stopped and studied it.

Crossbills sometimes sat in it, and on the pond rested coots, redheads, green-winged teals, buffleheads, gadwalls, and other waterfowl. Occasionally, in an alcove, sat a great horned owl.

And well we remember a pair of lady visitors who drove up to the museum and got out of their car. They looked around for a moment, up along the white cliffs, across the desert flats, and down toward the river bottom. Then one of them, with a frown, a sense of despair, and an air of pity, shook her head. "Whatever do you do out here," she asked, "all by yourself?"

Arches, Utah

A MODERN HIGHWAY SKIRTS THE SOUTHERN RAMPARTS of the Book Cliffs, and if a traveler heading west from Colorado yearns for something more than ribbons of roadway, he has a remarkable opportunity to veer off into some secret hideaways most people pass on by.

He hardly covers a mile before the spell of the old dirt road begins to grip him. All the roads of Utah were once like this, of course, but now they are no longer major routes. Just by turning off onto this road he eliminates at least a half of the world he knows, the world of superhighways.

He stops. What wonderful, delicious air! He takes in gulps of it to savor once again the taste of an atmosphere that is free and natural and that is fragrant with the spice of sage.

Cactus flowers across the plain shine a bright magenta, like little fires lit in the morning sun. He kneels to examine them: the multiple stamens, the fragile, pointed petals, the delicate needle designs, all existing without being seen or appreciated by any other organism except the insects that seek their nectar.

He walks. Without any special notion of where he is going, or what he will do when he gets there, he walks. And wonders. Why so much grass and so many flowers in a land of so little rain? Why such—

88

A lark flies up, sweeping high in the air, repeating its song that, faint though it is, seems amplified in the silence.

And then there is a bluff. The wanderer stands overlooking the broad brown valley of the Colorado River a hundred feet below. From the edge of the water, giant cottonwoods reach up the rocks as though to touch his feet.

Miles away, the red cliffs rise in the morning haze, and the massive river flows ponderously and powerfully toward them. Above the red cliffs stands the blue massif of the La Sal Mountains, outlined by patches of snow on their sides and summits.

The sun illuminates the whole landscape with a cheerful brilliance. So clear is the air, and so magnifying its effect, that objects a hundred miles away seem surely to require only a few hours' walk to reach.

From the branch of a cottonwood comes a flash of white and a raucous screech. A magpie asserts its dominance of this region, swooping down and across the surface of the muddy water and zooming up to perch in a lone cottonwood on the opposite bank.

Cicadas hum in the trees. The temperature rises. The horizon begins to waver in the heat.

The traveler finds his way back to his car. He has had an introduction to the Arches country. His mind is anything but at rest; it turns with thoughts of a nature different from those to which he is accustomed. He is eager to go on, to see more, to discover as much as he can. . . .

We have approached the Arches country from half a dozen directions, and it is nearly impossible to pick a favorite route. This one has the edge, however, because a dirt road slows you down, winds you around, takes you close to cliffs whose designs are infinitely compelling.

For example, as the road drops into moist bottomlands, we pass cliffs pocked with thousands of holes: little holes, big holes, long lines of holes, cavities, pits, gouges, as though the whole wall had once received a fusillade in some great Utah insurrection. But it is only the process of differential weathering, the uneven erosion of rock due to steady attack by the elements.

We saw piles of soil and traces of dunes along the bases of the cliffs. Obviously the red sandstone, everywhere around us, was disintegrating. At the edge of the Colorado River, where we crossed, grew banks of cottonwood and Tamarix, patches of oak and copses of willow, but their roots did not bind the banks for long. Chunks of rock that had once been part of the cliffs above lay strewn all along, and would soon be dismantled by ice and water and wind. They had, in fact, been part of the layer of sandstone that covered this region millenniums ago to a thickness of unknown hundreds of feet.

The river itself was the same color as the cliffs. Muddy, sandy, silty, it was simply cliffs going downriver, cliffs reduced to dust, cliffs pulverized to particles that would remain suspended in water, cliffs being carried away by floods as fast as they could be transported down the canyons and dumped into the river.

Floods? Not on a morning like this! The sky so clear, the sun so bright, the breeze so gentle—there was not the slightest hint of violence. Yet across the plateaus and along the river terraces lay evidence of past cloudbursts that had torn away the sands and pebbles and rock and rolled them to the river's edge.

The canyon closed in. The cliffs grew higher. The sun beat into the narrow, winding gorge with the maximum intensity of midday. Magpies commuted from place to place in the cottonwood community, and a ground squirrel came out of its burrow, sat up, turned, and assumed a sentinel's pose.

Around the bend we came to a view of Fisher Towers, an isolated set of sandstone obelisks at the edge of a red plateau. Along the river, purple-flowered Tamarix waved their limbs.

It would have been tempting to stop and spend a week searching out the secrets of the cottonwood groves—cicadas sang, magpies called, swifts flew in and out among the crags, vultures patrolled the sky.

But had we stopped everywhere we wished—and it was always easy to get sidetracked in eastern Utah—we would never have reached the Arches. The temptation of seeing them again exceeded all else.

Proceeding through cuts in the Entrada sandstone, a massive brown rock that seemed to say that the world was solid and stable and everlasting, we knew we were getting closer to the great panoramas of stone.

And then, at last, Park Avenue, a gorge flanked by massive walls and thick-shouldered promontories, where the whole conception of terra firma seemed confirmed.

ARCHES NATIONAL MONUMENT, UTAH:
top–Fisher Towers;
right–dead juniper tree;
far right, top–wall face
pocked by differential weathering;
far right, bottom–sheer walls of Park Avenue

Those great walls, as anyone could see, were as solid as any marble building man had erected; they had obviously been there for centuries.

But presently one's eyes begin to observe contradictory evidence. Spilled out on the Carmel formation below are chunks of Entrada sandstone that look as though they had fallen yesterday or the day before. Up on the ledges lie other boulders that seem to need only a gentle push to send them off.

Where ancient bedding planes of dunes that formed the Entrada meet, a series of little erosion pockets have formed, and they look as though a giant woodpecker once clambered along the cliff and pecked out rows of holes at different levels.

Mostly sheer, the walls of Park Avenue are slender, little more than upright slabs. In the recent past thin, waferlike chunks have fallen from them and shattered on the rocks below.

All these were manifestations of a temporary landscape, not a permanent one, terra "infirma" rather than "firma." Everywhere we looked the landscape lay in ruin. Pinnacles, columns, hummocks, abutments, and domes had been produced in nearly every size and shape by erosion. Each had a different design, was striped either horizontally or vertically or both by colors in the rock or by the stains from rains that poured down over the edge.

Other cliffs were slit in ways that resembled the gills of fish. Strange friezes stretched along the rims and cornices, indiscriminately cut by the cracking of rock, carved by moving water, and buffed by grains of sand borne on the wind.

Going down through Courthouse Wash and up the undulating incline on the other side we saw new evidence of instability of the land. Over there were two abutments from which had probably fallen a great rock span that must have once looked exceedingly strong and massive. There were sites of fallen arches, and giant boulders perched on pedestals, somewhat out of balance, ready to topple.

The mind is boggled by the progression of shapes that now appear, many more than ever suspected from a distance. Coves and promontories seem to leap into the sky at our approach; windows and open holes and slots in the rock become evident. There are tunnels, potholes, overhangs, fins, fin canyons, turrets.

Although we see only a few openings at a time, the rocks of this region are perforated with thousands of holes. Earth movements have so cracked the

Entrada sandstone as to slice it thinly with joints and fractures. Along these joints erosion, chiefly by running or freezing water, has cut narrowly and deeply. The wider the water cuts the canyons, the more slender grow the walls between.

Since the underlying Carmel formation is soft and usually erodes at a faster rate, it undermines the Entrada walls, which then break away in cliffs. Eventually, at a weak point in the wall, an opening occurs, is widened, and becomes an arch. This area of Utah possesses probably the greatest concentration of arches in the world.

Counting every opening that exceeds ten feet in diameter as one worth recognizing, then the 129 square miles of Arches National Monument contain at least 88 arches. More may be found as explorations continue; there is such a maze of canyons that a great deal of effort will be required to find them all.

Some of the arches are enormous. The largest opening in Double Arch is 160 feet in diameter. There are tunnel arches, turret arches, and alcove arches, some so close together that they appear to be a parade of elephants etched in solid rock. Landscape Arch, believed to be the longest natural-stone span in the world, measures 291 feet between buttresses. Fortunately there are no major earth movements today; damaging earthquakes here are virtually unknown.

Delicate Arch is the finest and most fragile. You must hike to it to get the full effect, and the hike itself is a part of the grand adventure. After climbing for nearly two miles over rounded sandstone slopes and through gullies graced with juniper you make the final ascent along a trail cut into the cliff. The view is, in a way, unsurpassed in the region, for there is the arch, some 65 feet in height, shaped like an inverted parabola, and through it may be seen the La Sal Mountains. At the edge of a sunken, slick rock amphitheater it stands as though it were some ceremonial arch beneath which the gods will receive an incantation.

To some visitors, alas, this is the culmination of a visit to the Arches; their motto seems to be "See Delicate Arch and Go." And having gone, they are satisfied they have seen all that is necessary, and that any more could only be anticlimactic.

But they have not emerged from their cars and gone out among the fins and felt the cool wind blowing beneath the walls of the canyons. They have not paused long enough to see the flowers of desert-plume highlighted by the sun against the shadows of an alcove, looking like tiny rockets leaping skyward.

They cannot have had time to learn the secret of Salt Valley, which lies on an enormous dome of common table salt. For this valley is on the surface of a giant salt dome, one of many such geologic structures in the world. Saline rocks such as salt and gypsum have, over the millenniums, been covered by sediment, eroded, and covered again; they have adjusted and readjusted their configuration many times in response to varying pressures within the earth. Ground water has dissolved some of these salt masses, which has caused parts of the surface to collapse. Thus basins like this literally float on deep deposits of salt.

And unless visitors have a topographic map they cannot see how strangely Salt Valley is aligned with Paradox Valley, on the far side of the La Sal Mountains, 45 miles away; and with half a dozen other depressions in eastern Utah and western Colorado.

The abundance of salts accounts for the potash mines in the vicinity, but out at the Arches there are no mines or miners. Silence, freedom, and natural beauty exist not only on a giant scale but on a personal and intimate one. We climbed by ropes one day to a tiny tank tucked in a hidden vale above Park Avenue. In western parlance a "tank" is a place where water gathers, and here we found a basin on which weathering agents had been at work for centuries.

A great deal of life exists in such pools perched high on the barren rock, but the water does not remain forever; the pools dry up and muddy sediment on the bottom shrivels and cracks. A lone cottonwood at the edge of the pool unfurls its leaves, but the grass has only a brief hegemony, and shortly withers.

Back in hidden canyons lie what the hurried traveler may always have yearned to find: a paradise on earth. If he would leave his car and walk up certain sandy washes, he might round a corner and find at his feet a flow of water, a grassy bank, and a copse of cottonwoods.

Through the woods a short way, he would come to what surely must be the loveliest pool on earth, a pond fed by seeps coming down the wall of an enclosing amphitheater perhaps a hundred feet in diameter. Waters have dissolved the alcove, and still may enlarge it a little through floods from each summer cloudburst.

As he arrives, the hiker encounters moist, cool air that laves his baked and desiccated skin. Sunlight falls through the cottonwood leaves and drops to the surface of the clear pool. There its light is reflected up into shadows that cover the curving wall of the cove. As patches of light dance on the surface of the water, so splotches of light on the shadowed wall break into pieces and come together again. They split and explode and dash across the banks of fern and moss and primrose and mimulus, shining into the clusters of reddish monkey flowers that suddenly, fleetingly, look like flashes of fire on the walls.

Down along hanging gardens of moss and fern the seeping water makes its way, poises for a moment, soaking up sunlight like diamonds suspended in air, then falls.

Striking the surface, the drops of water generate delicate, bell-like tones that are reinforced by the acoustics of the chamber. Another drop falls. Another bell rings. Another flurry of flashing lights streaks through the shadows and back again.

But the traveler has waited enough. It is off with his clothes and into the water, sinking, reveling, cooling, splashing, losing all track of time, knowing only the ringing reality of the falling water, or the silence of the depths beneath. The overhang and the soft green leaves shut out the fiercest rays of the drying sun. No sound, not even the call of the magpie, distracts from the music of this experience. He leaps. He swims. He splashes. He is free.

The dry breeze finally lifts from his skin the drops of precious moisture. He dresses and goes back out through the cottonwoods and along the grassy banks to the stream. He may walk for a while without shoes, and splash along in the water, sinking to his ankles in the mud and thinking of the almost forgotten time when he used to do this kind of thing every day in summer.

The sun sinks lower. The heat blasts by reflection directly into his face. The sun burns into his neck and arms. Too much sun and too much distance, of course, can lead to danger and disaster, for the desert can sneak up mercilessly. The temperature can rise to more than 110 degrees in summer. To achieve the feeling of freedom that now possesses him, he has had to bury himself in this sculptured desert wilderness, but he knows he could get lost. So he keeps to the stream, never straying very far from it.

The walk back does not take long. He has not been out here more than a couple of hours; at the most he was hardly three miles from the road.

He spies his car in the distance. With that, the shackles of time and civilization again snap into place. For a while his soul was in flight, and he was completely free of those shackles. Some day he will come back to his "sleepy hollow," or find another—this region has several of them—and there he will devote as many hours as possible to the joy of living.

Thus in places like the Arches, travelers can take more advantage of the land than they may realize—providing they do it on nature's terms. Not everyone, however, is equipped to understand or appreciate—to "get their good tidings" as John Muir might have said if he had seen the Arches.

One simply must detach himself and go, whether or not the horizon is promising.

Near Delicate Arch, for example, is a typical red-rock desert stream called Salt Wash. It does not look like much where we enter it, for the low hills bordering the stream are not impressive. But around a couple of bends, the cliffs close in, and from that point on the place is a delight.

Rounded slopes of red sandstone, trying to nurture a juniper here and there, curve about as though their contours had been conceived by random strokes of an architect's brush. These cornices come down to the river terrace, which is crowded with cottonwood and willow, and the terrace in turn gives way to the sandy bottom of the stream. The sand is wet and we see the tracks of limbs that were dragged across the sand. Mingled with these lines are tracks of beavers who cut and carried the trees downstream.

On several occasions, we have made our way through tangles of Tamarix and seepwillow, avoiding prominent patches of poison ivy, and found a spring at the base of a water-stained wall. We slid into the hidden pool, along with frogs and water beetles and fragments of leaves carried down from trees or shrubs out of sight above.

When we think of Salt Wash now, it is with a smile and a fancy that no one else knows anything about it. That is not the case, of course, but there have never been any other persons along the wash on the days we spent there.

No matter how many days have been allocated for a visit to the Arches,

Johns Hopkins Glacier and
12,726-foot Mount Crillon of the Fairweather Range,
Glacier Bay National Monument, Alaska

Fireweed at Glacier Bay National Monument, Alaska.
Right–Ponderosa pine forest in the Eagle Nest Butte region,
Lava Beds National Monument, California

Place of Refuge at Honaunau, City of Refuge
National Historical Park, island of Hawaii, Hawaii.
Right–Montezuma Well, Montezuma Castle
National Monument, Arizona

Cactus flowers common at Arches National Monument, Utah.
Right–Double Arch, Arches National Monument

Mississippi River as seen from Fire Point Trail,
Effigy Mounds National Monument, Iowa.
Right–H. L. Dousman's office on the grounds of his estate,
Villa Louis, Prairie du Chien, Wisconsin

Flower cluster of African tulip tree
in Caribbean National Forest, Puerto Rico.
Right—Luquillo Beach, on Atlantic Ocean shore, Puerto Rico
(3,494-foot El Yunque in background)

Pleasant Pond Stream, east of
the Carry Ponds, Maine.
Right–Maple leaves on forest floor, Maine

Mushrooms near Quantico Creek.
Right–Prince William Forest Park, Virginia,
Quantico Creek

Water tupelo and bald cypress swamp
near Natchez Trace Parkway,
Mississippi section

time always falls short. Coming back past the junction to Park Avenue, we stop, almost nostalgically, to see this grand gorge once again, to view it in late afternoon light—only to find that it has utterly changed. What was shadowed in morning now glows in the light of the late evening sun. The friezes that stood out sharply earlier have faded into the oblivion of evening shadow. Indeed, new sculptures not even noticed before have sprung into prominence.

Sun lights the western fin wall from behind, illuminating it in the same way that sometimes gives a cloud a silver lining. Those pinnacles that seemed rather flat in the morning are now silhouetted boldly against the glare of the sun. The junipers below are engulfed in shadow.

Thus the mind is enlarged by scenes made different with the time of day. If to these are added the moods of weather and moods of season, it is obvious that every visit here is different.

And it would take a good many visits to explore even half of the hidden recesses in this complicated sandstone wilderness. The Fiery Furnace, for example, is quite literally a maze of fin canyons in which the unprepared newcomer could get lost for days. A guided loop trail leads into it part way, and one can also circulate around the fringes and penetrate into the narrow avenues for short distances.

Once inside, the walls close in overhead so that there is only a narrow slit of sky. In places we may touch both walls at once, or we walk among trees fitted snugly into the rocky corridors.

A breeze comes into the narrow defile from the flats beyond the canyon mouth. In such natural chutes the wind is almost always restless, shaping and reshaping the dunes that have been blown against the lower rock walls, and causing the abrasive particles to polish the rock.

In places sandstone blocks have broken and fallen from cliffs above and exploded on impact, lying where they fell—but only temporarily as disintegration of the land goes on.

For an hour or two the sun will spill its rays into this deep defile, and then be gone. In times of heavy rain, the collected waters will rise and gather everything that is loose and roar around each corner until departing at some distant exit.

Perhaps this is the greatest lesson and most obvious secret of the Arches —that solid land, and therefore everything, is only temporary. While at first the massive sandstone walls seemed stable and looked as though they could never fall, we now see that they are coming down. Bit by bit, piece by piece, they fall, even within the memory of man. In 1940 a chunk fell out of Skyline Arch. In 1962 a sizeable portion of cliff fell near the Double Arch. And in 1969 a large piece fell from Wall Arch.

The geologist sees this all quite clearly, for he has dealt in millions of years instead of in human lifetimes. Now greater numbers of people are becoming aware of the lengths of time involved and of the inherent fascination of the earth's stone layers; the most popular exhibit in the Arches National Monument Visitor Center is a columnar collection of the dozen or so rock layers to be found within the area. Thus the celebrated geologist, Grove Karl Gilbert, who participated in scientific surveys of this region a century ago, when it was really secret, would happily find some kindred spirits today who understood one of the central thoughts of his work: "The geologist has ceased to look upon the present order of things as an ultimate result, and has come to perceive that the epoch in which he lives is a geological epoch, that geological history as well as human history is enacting, and that the earth has a future no less than a past."

Because the land is so fragile, one comes away from the Arches with a disturbing question: How much can man mar it?

It would be quite easy to ruin the effect of what was intended by law. To conserve the features unimpaired for the benefit and enjoyment of future generations is the general mandate; the original proclamation, signed by President Hoover in 1929, calls for preservation of the Arches and other features for their educational and scenic value.

Some persons say that any road into the heart of this delicate wonderland is a tasteless infringement upon the sensibilities of thinking human beings, and time will probably prove them right. There is little doubt in our minds that the Arches are better discovered on foot, without mechanical contrivances.

Even so, this national monument stands as an example of human restraint in an era of superdevelopment. In a region where trees are few, the land open, and geological features the major resource, man has attempted to harmonize his works with those of nature. The monument visitor center is a relatively inconspicuous building that presents a low profile and a blending color at the entrance to the site. The road that climbs the cliff just beyond has been so constructed that it is virtually invisible from the ground below. Any scars have been camouflaged or removed.

Farther on, the highway curves past features of interest in such a way that nowhere does one see very much of the road ahead. At present, the pavement reaches the Windows section and Devils Garden, which is about the maximum mileage intended. The federal government, for once, has said that development is complete, and that to reach the unseen wonders you must get out of your car and set off on foot.

Perhaps the next generation will decide that even this much development is too much. They may insist on removal of the campground, for example, considering campgrounds unnecessary and undesirable in any national preserve because each precious square inch of land was set aside for purposes of natural beauty, quiet, and inspiration.

We are already seeing the vindication of restraint as a triumph of tourism—a nonconsumptive industry—over the extractive industries. Local people still believe that potash and uranium mines were the ultimate salvation of the region because the benefits of those industries could be measured in payrolls.

Now tourism has grown into an industry itself, with little likelihood of running dry because the resource is inexhaustible. If the scenery is kept free of pollution and tramways, if an overabundance of tourists can be controlled by limiting the number of persons who can enter the Arches country at any one time, and if the roads can indeed be reduced, then the ecosystems should remain intact for future use.

In any case, tourism itself is measured in payrolls now—food, lodging, souvenirs, transportation. In ten years, the city of Moab has added some 14 gasoline stations and two motels to its streets, and is growing in a way that some of the early inhabitants may have expected it to boom from uranium alone.

Out of respect to the wonders of the earth, man has preserved a place where geological history, like human history, is still progressing, and where the earth has a future no less than a past. That means that if our descendants would like to go looking for their own "sleepy hollows" and the secrets of their own salt washes, here is a good place to start.

The MIDWEST and SOUTH

❧ The MIDWEST and SOUTH

ACROSS THE CENTRAL LOWLANDS AND SPREADING PLAINS of North America, one relies less on sandstone cliffs, towering peaks, and plunging canyons for natural wonder than on the infinite subtleties of nature. Indeed, the beauties of the Midwest and South take on a special grandeur, a different grandeur, an unexpected grandeur by the combination of their gentle qualities.

The fantastic, said Clarence E. Dutton, pioneer Western geologist, is only momentarily arresting. Human beings tend to prefer their interviews with nature on more intimate terms. Broad sweeps of wilderness, even in the West, are but introductory. In the Midwest and South, men reserve their more permanent affections for a sunlit forest glade, a prairie swale, a bayou caressed by salted winds, a river slough, or a quiet pond in a northern wood.

The Midwest and South are full of color. One does not soon forget the brilliant pink of wild roses climbing across the face of a purple quartzite cliff in Minnesota. It is a land of deciduous forests, and with the coming of fall there is a display parallel to that of the aspen in the West, yet vastly different. In the Ozarks we have passed more than one autumn watching the grand procession of green dissolving to reveal the latent yellows, oranges, and reds, and then these turning to russet and falling to the forest floor.

The famed pipestone quarry of Minnesota has been dug into a handsome red shale called catlinite, from which the Indians fashioned their social pipes and pipes of peace, the great calumets of aboriginal history and legend.

In the South are delicate cream and orange of both magnolia and honeysuckle, the rich red soils of mining country, the chocolate rivers, the green and yellow canopy of leaves that illuminate somber swamps like a skylight in a gallery of art.

Thousands of scenes are stored in our memories, retrievable scenes of quiet, colorful woods invested with dankness, decay, and growth, or of blue pools along such rivers as the Gasconade and Big Piney in Missouri. At each retrieval, these scenes leap into life: We swing on a vine, in a high, long arc through the air, and plunge toward the quiet surface of the water; the picture explodes in a splash, and suddenly there is a different silence. We sink into a liquid dimension of dimly lighted green, where roots and trailing curtains of algae, together with floating leaves and furious flights of fish, are the constituents of another world more secret than the one in which we live.

Between Canada and Mexico, a traveler with perception is bound to have some lasting memory of a pond or vale or shady grove that somehow struck him right and made him pause on a busy day. That pond, that vale, that grove henceforth belongs to him, and perhaps to a thousand other human beings, unknown to him. Someone else, of course, may hold a legal title to his pond or vale, but no law bars his borrowing inspiration from the place, or telling friends about it, or recalling the freshness and purity of it on wintry days when he is chambered and insulated at home.

Or even in admiration of his own kind, he finds in the Midwest and South the stimuli that show how much worth living life is. The central lowlands are full of historic images—not only of prairies and plains and forests, but of thundering herds of bison and of galloping Indian ponies.

The region springs alive with the adventures of fur traders in their canoes piled high with pelts, of military explorers, of southern traders sweeping the Spanish moss from their eyes as they rode through the sweet luxuriance of delta forests. Through all of these scenes, both physically and chronologically, threads that one great entity to which nearly everything else was bound in the heart of the continent: the Mississippi River and its tributary systems. Little in history or prehistory has transpired without this river being involved, directly or indirectly. It forms, in a way, the thread of coherence that links the secret places of today with the secret, timeless past of the old Midwest and the antebellum South.

In the two chapters that follow, we share a few surprises that came our way while on quests of different kinds. Both involve distinguished men and their ladies. And both involve a great many men whose names have become lost in antiquity.

One takes in the North, and one the South. Each demonstrates how men today can become completely absorbed in what went on in the different worlds from which our present-day civilization sprang.

Prairie du Chien, Wisconsin 🌿

I<small>T CAME AS AN ASSIGNMENT ONE EXPECTS LITTLE OF: SPEND</small> a month preparing development plans for a seemingly obscure collection of Indian mounds in a place that time had passed and forgotten.

The ancient mounds of America are not, in a number of ways, as bold and dramatic as the cliff dwellings of the old Southwest. They are certainly widespread; men have been building mounds of one sort or another, primarily for the burial of the dead, for as long as history has been recorded, and are still doing it—the gravestones and monuments of cemeteries are simply modifications.

"Mounds are among the earliest and most widely distributed memorials of the dead," said noted archaeologist Gerard Fowke. "Savages could pile up earth and stone before they could carve a rock or hew a piece of wood. . . . Nothing is more enduring; and when settled into compactness and covered with sod, a heap of earth will remain unchanged through vicissitudes that reduce to ruins any other product of human industry. It is expected, then, that such tumuli would be of world-wide occurrence. . . ."

They are—in Central and South America, across Europe, Asia, northern

Africa, and in North America throughout most of the South and Midwest.

But to a good many travelers, a mound is a mound, and hardly something to get excited about. One reason is that mounds are low and rounded and inconspicuous. True enough, there are assorted shapes and sizes—the snakelike Great Serpent Mound of Ohio, for example—but one almost needs a helicopter to rise high enough for a clear, perspective view.

Thus it was not an assignment full of promise to spend a month at Iowa's Effigy Mounds National Monument, across the Mississippi from Prairie du Chien, Wisconsin. Yet before we were through we would be involved with two presidents, a host of Indian chiefs, battles, massacres, medical experiments of a bizarre nature, burial grounds, famous explorers, iceboats, a celebrated conservationist, a river, and a mystery of missing glaciers.

On approaching the Effigy Mounds region, one sinks into valleys and glens, and soon finds himself among buttes and cliffs, and when he arrives at the Mississippi he moves beneath bluffs that are several hundred feet high.

This should not be; after all, the Midwest is gently rolling terrain, for the most part lacking prominent features. Yet here is a rugged land, a "driftless area," so called because the great ice sheets that once dumped glacial debris, or drift, so widely elsewhere did not here.

Much of the Midwest is buried in drift to a thickness of over a thousand feet. The rich black soils have been widely put to agricultural uses. But here at the junction of Wisconsin, Iowa, and Minnesota, 20,000 square miles of relatively undisturbed landscape remain, unscathed by glaciation either because it lay in the lee of a highland that might have diverted the southward movement of ice, or because the ice sheets never quite coalesced in this region.

The driftless area is not entirely driftless (there are a few glacial deposits here and there), but it was essentially untouched by ice, and therein lies a part of its charm today.

Through these valleys and among the ridges have coursed the Mississippi and its tributaries for centuries, rising and falling with the fluvial cycle, aggrading and degrading, laying down floodplains that were later called "prairies" by early human explorers. Most of these, however, became heavily wooded and not like open prairies farther west.

Prairies, bluffs, rivers, woods—such was the home of the ancient Mound Builders. Of these Indian tribes too little is known to postulate adequately all aspects of their lives and times. They were chiefly hunters, gatherers, and fisher-men, and a limited agriculture did exist in later periods, but what they thought and how they arranged their daily family and social affairs is lost through their lack of a written language.

The major evidence of their occupation is a system of 15,000 Indian mounds in Wisconsin. About a third of this number are unique because of their shape. Most of the effigy mounds of the world are found in southern Wisconsin and parts of adjacent states. They date from approximately a thousand years ago.

Throughout the effigy area are mounds constructed to resemble lizards, panthers, turtles, bears, bison, beaver, geese, and eagles. One in the shape of a man has been found. Some mounds are 6 feet high, some more than 600 feet in length. In addition to the effigy forms are conical and linear mounds, as well as combinations of these two.

Whatever compelled the Indians to build their mounds in the shapes of animals? Was it art? Religion? Tradition? Burials were located at various levels in the mounds, and usually in the region of the heart or the head or the flank. When buried in effigy mounds, the dead were sometimes laid out flat, but more commonly—after decomposition of the body on a ceremonial scaffold—their bones were collected into bundles. One mound in Marquette County, Wisconsin, con-tained 45 bundle burials.

Few objects were buried with the dead, yet these people must have been as vain as any, and probably wore strings of beads and related ornaments. In any case, the Mound Builders went to considerable labor in preparing a place for the bones. And without shovels or wheelbarrows, the building of these mounds was not very easy.

Birch-bark buckets or baskets were probably the major means of convey-ing earth from one site to another. The task could conceivably have been a ceremonial and community one. Indeed, if the effigy Mound Builders belonged to bird and bear clans, as some modern tribes still do, that is perhaps the reason for the shapes of the mounds. They were quite an innovation, if so.

In the end, we are left with more mysteries about the mounds than we shall ever unravel. At some point in their history, long before the arrival of European explorers, these ancient Indians ceased building their sacred effigy mounds.

We do not know what happened to the tribes as a whole. Their line of descent may have come down to historic times through Ioway, Menominee, and Potawatomi people. But these Indians had lost all knowledge about the Mound Builders and the meaning of the effigies.

And so we had discovered that there were extraordinary shapes and designs half hidden in these bluff-top forests, and their presence led to a host of silent secrets that opened a world of speculation.

The more we delved into what had occurred in this region, the more it began to appear that a lively sequence of events had taken place here. A short distance down the Mississippi and across on the other side, the Wisconsin River comes from the hinterlands to pour its collected tribute into the Father of Waters. Down that tributary, in 1673, came two white-skinned explorers where only red-skinned ones had come before. In the middle of June, in birch-bark canoes, arrived two men who have become well remembered in the European exploration of the continent: Louis Jolliet, 24, commissioned to extend the domain of France as far as he could, and the Reverend Jacques Marquette, S.J., 36, founder of a mission at Saint Ignace on the north shore of the Straits of Mackinac.

The immediate aim of both was to discover the great western river about which they had heard from the Indians, and when they did, Marquette was filled "with a joy that I cannot express."

Such joys today are hard to explain, because on high-speed highways we cross so many rivers we scarcely notice them. But if we imagine ourselves to be miles from the last outpost of civilization, in a frail canoe on the wilderness frontier, when spring has arrived and the leaves have enlarged and thickened and are about to take on the rich dark green of summer, then we shall be closer to that historic day in 1673.

From the bluffs of Wisconsin's Wyalusing State Park, we may stand as an Indian might have on that day, and see the Wisconsin River below, still lined with heavy forest, wide and placid as it joins the wider and also placid Mississippi.

White men's canoes came in increasing numbers as the years went on. But, alas, it was exploitation of Indian country that became the central aim.

The Illinois, Chippewa, Sioux, Menominee, Sauk, Fox, and Winnebago, obedient to the ecosystems that supported them, bore the brunt of this commercial attack, and times began to change. Trading fleets penetrated the interior, and animal pelts came out by the hundreds of thousands.

About 1754 the first white settler, Jean Marie Cardinal, took up life with his wife and a Mandan Indian slave on the prairie just north of the confluence of the Wisconsin and Mississippi rivers.

At this stage the land was still unquestionably Indian, and any settler, French or otherwise, established life and liberty only at the sufferance of the Indians. Traffic increased and the flat land at the junction of the rivers—the "prairie"—became an active rendezvous point in an age when rivers were the only routes of transportation. Eventually the site, this flat border of the river, got its name from Alim of Big Dog, chief of a Fox Indian village along the river; hence, Prairie du Chien, "Prairie of the Dog."

As a trader of the time described it:

I . . . Desended the River to the Mouth which Emteys into the Masseippy and Cros that River and Incampt . . . next Morning we Recrost ye River which was about a Mile Brod and Mounted about three Miles til we Come to the Planes of the Dogs. . . . Hear we Meat a Larg Number of french and Indans Makeing out thare arrangements for the InSewing winter and sending of thare cannoes to Differant Parts—Like wise Giveing Creadets to the Indans who were all to Rondoveuse thare in Spring. . . .

To be Intelagabel I Go back to the Planes of the Dogs . . . this Plane is a Very Handsum one Which is on the East side of the River on the Pint of Land Betwene the Mouth of Wisconstan whare it Emties in to the Masseppey & the Last River. The Plane is Verey Smooth hear. All the traders that Youseis that Part of the Countrey & all the Indans of Several tribes Meat fall & Spring whare the Grateist Games are Plaid Both by french & Indans.

Prairie du Chien was also used by the British as a site from which to launch attacks against Americans and Spanish. Yet the real and enduring attack was against the Indians, to take their land one way or another, to usurp,

PRAIRIE DU CHIEN, WISCONSIN:
right–window at Villa Louis;
bottom–blockhouse of Old Fort Crawford;
far right–chapel in Villa Louis

encroaching bit by bit, until the spreading hordes of newcomers became as ubiquitous as the Indian. Land grants were often made without considering to which
Indian tribe the land belonged. White men seemed to assume that the land was
theirs for the taking.

French, Spanish, and British traders worked in and out of Prairie du
Chien, but John Jacob Astor's American Fur Company ultimately played the
dominant role.

The traders bought and sold all manner of things besides fur, of course.
Their object was to make as much money as possible by creating and supply-
ing the wants of the Indians and obtaining whatever they could in return. They
dealt in such commodities as cattle, feathers, lead, wheat, oats, peas, flour, meats,
ginseng, and dry goods.

By the early 1820s the American Fur Company had thousands of *voy-
ageurs* and hundreds of clerks throughout its domain, and was dispensing pelts
by the hundreds of thousands at New York auctions.

In those early days of the fledgling United States there was not only
competition from British traders but so many lawless elements on a wild frontier that one would expect the army to assert its protection early. It did. And
the first evidence of it adds another famous name to the *dramatis personae* of
historic events at Prairie du Chien.

In 1805 Lt. Zebulon Pike, with 20 men in a keelboat, departed Saint Louis
with orders to explore the Mississippi to its source. After almost a month heading north on the river, he arrived at Prairie du Chien and during the course of
explorations on the opposite side of the Mississippi, across from the mouth of
the Wisconsin River, he climbed a 500-foot-high ridge. The ridge itself commanded a splendid view of this strategic river junction; it was level and had
a spring behind, an excellent location for a military post, so Pike marked some
trees at the site.

For a long time the ridge was called Pike's Hill; today it is Pikes Peak
State Park, property of the State of Iowa. From the ridge a visitor sees approximately what Pike saw. If, in his imagination, he removes the distant bridge
across the Wisconsin, he might as well be Pike, scanning the forests, assessing
the value of the waterways, studying the timber resources, the vales, the ground

beneath his feet. No fort exists, as Pike would have had it, but redheaded wood-peckers seem to guard the forest, flying, drilling, and calling among the tall oaks each summer morning.

Pike spent the winter in the upper reaches of the Mississippi, and on re-turning downstream in the spring of 1806 he spent five days at Prairie du Chien. Later on, of course, he discovered in what is now Colorado the towering, snow-covered peak that also bears his name.

In such ways is Prairie du Chien linked to other times and other places.

Scarcely six years later, another figure well known in United States his-tory became directly involved here. It was Maj. Zachary Taylor, who ordered a detachment of troops to Prairie du Chien in 1814 to build a fort for protec-tion against the British, with whom the country was then at war. Named Fort Shelby, it was built on an old Indian mound, one of many in this region, just behind the village and a stone's throw from the Mississippi River. It did not last long. The British attacked it in due course, took it, occupied it, changed its name to Fort McKay, and, the following year, burned it.

By that time the war was over anyway, and so were years of interna-tional strife along the frontier. Yet here at the edge of Indian territory, the need for a fort was considered crucial, which accounts for the building of Fort Crawford. Indeed, the Indians had begun to protest vigorously the encroachments upon their terrain, the "aggression of the whites," as it has been called.

At times Prairie du Chien must have seemed like an island in a sea of hostility, and courageous were the souls of those who went to serve there.

In 1825, for example, the whole plain north of the village was filled with Indians who had come to discuss in council their tribal boundaries. Imagine the sight and the sound! Army officers in full dress uniforms, Indians in elegant buf-falo robes, Indians wearing or carrying knives, clubs, lances, red stone pipes, and feather flags, cannons firing, drums beating, chiefs orating, people shouting, dogs barking, and the smell of smoke and of meat cooking.

It was the greatest gathering of tribes that had ever occurred, said Henry Rowe Schoolcraft, pioneer American ethnologist. "We found a very large number of various tribes assembled," he wrote. "Not only the village, but the entire banks of the river for miles above and below the town, and the island in the river, [were] covered with their tents. The Dakotahs, with their high-pointed buffalo skin tents . . . and their decorations and implements of flags, feathers, skins and personal 'braveries,' presented the scene of a Bedouin encampment."

There were Yankton, Winnebago, Chippewa, Menominee, Iroquois, Ioway, Sauk, Fox. Some had tufts of red horsehair tied at their elbows and wore necklaces of grizzly bear claws. Their heads were largely shaved and painted.

"Keokuk," said Schoolcraft, "stood with his war lance, high crest of feathers, and daring eye, like another Coriolanus, and when he spoke in council, and at the same time shook his lance at his enemies, the Sioux, it was evident that he wanted but an opportunity to make their blood flow like water."

The treaty council had been called to work out boundary lines between tribes, thus hopefully bringing more peace to the frontier, and involved work with bark maps and drawings, orations on all sides, and seemingly endless negotiations that dragged on for a month.

But in the end the Treaty of 1825 worked to the advantage of the newcomers. With the convening of other councils it became quite clear that the white man was no brother, but rather bent on buying or taking so much Indian land as to disintegrate the red man's territory. Concessions, gifts, money, services: the Indians soon wound up with a greater past than future. In due time they were pushed so far to the west, with their claims to land extinguished and their former territory closed, that Prairie du Chien ceased being important as a central council site.

The situation is summed up by the capture of Chief Red Bird, at Prairie du Chien.

"I am ready," he said, surveying the American troops and stepping forward. "I do not wish to be put in irons; let me be free. I have given away my life; it is gone—" he stooped and took some dust between his thumb and finger, blowing it away "—like that."

He watched the dust as it fell.

"I would not take it back; it is gone."

As time went on, the settlers at Prairie du Chien knew terror, scalpings, and killings at the hands of disgruntled Indians, thus continuing the justification for Fort Crawford, and for a good many years it was the principal military post on the upper Mississippi.

Or *in* the Mississippi. When floods came and water rose over the river-bank, the buildings became half submerged. With that, decay set in, and a few years later a new Fort Crawford was built at a higher site and farther from the river.

It was also of higher quality, being constructed of stone, and having a hospital, magazine, gunhouse, store, barracks, officers' quarters, and so on.

The army had plenty to do. At times it drove settlers out of Indian lands, but things were often the other way around, and the spinning cycle of Indian wars went on.

The Black Hawk War, in the words of one historian, was a series of skirmishes against an enemy who twice tried in vain to surrender. Black Hawk, leader of the Sauk and Fox Indians, finally managed to give himself up and was delivered to Zachary Taylor, who had taken command at Fort Crawford, and was kept prisoner until he could be moved south.

And who took him south? None other than 2d Lt. Jefferson Davis, who apparently formed a close friendship with him.

What was this young man, who afterward became a United States senator and president of the Confederacy, doing at Fort Crawford? He himself says that he was in this region primarily "to watch the Indians who were semi-hostile, to prevent trespassing on Indian territory." He was not actually involved in the Black Hawk War because he had been on leave of absence.

Coincident with all this, one of the great milestones in medical history was established at Fort Crawford. It was here that the earliest and some of the most dramatic experiments were made in human physiology. We are hardly surprised, of course, that in such violent times there should have been an ample supply of injuries to study. What with scalps occasionally laid open, torsos ripped by musket fire, or physiques pierced by arrows, one could expect a field day for physicians. The trouble was that such injuries often resulted in the death of the victim and consequent cessation of bodily functions which the physiologist would have liked to observe in action.

On June 6, 1822, an 18-year-old French Canadian named Alexis St. Martin was accidentally ripped open by a musket blast at short range near Fort Mackinac, in Michigan Territory. The shot tore away a rib, part of the lower lung, and the left end of the stomach. When St. Martin was brought in to the post surgeon, a virtually unknown doctor named William Beaumont, he was treated and patched up as well as could be expected under the conditions, and given 36 hours to live.

He did much better than that because the gaping wound actually healed. But the hole in St. Martin's stomach never closed, and to Dr. Beaumont the opportunity this presented was too good to let slip by. The patient, with a compress over his wound, came to be known as the man with a lid on his stomach. In short, Beaumont had a miracle at his command.

St. Martin ultimately married, sired several children, and lived to be 83 years old. Between 1825 and 1833, off and on, Beaumont performed a series of 238 observations and experiments on him, both in Mackinac and in Prairie du Chien, where Beaumont became post surgeon at the Fort Crawford hospital. The experiments dealt essentially with digestion, and marked the first time that men ever discerned the gastric processes by direct observation.

In one experiment, Beaumont inserted into St. Martin's stomach a raw oyster affixed to a string so that it could be pulled out at intervals and examined. After half an hour, only the surface of the oyster was digested. At one hour, a third was digested but it still retained its shape. An hour and a half later the oyster was gone from the string, and in three hours the stomach was empty again.

Here is a typical experiment at Fort Crawford:

Experiment 12. March 13, 1830. At 10 o'clock, A.M.—stomach empty—introduced tube; but was unable to obtain any gastric juice. On the application of a few crumbs of bread to the inner surface of the stomach, the juice began slowly to accumulate, and flow through the tube. The crumbs of bread adhered to the mucous coat, soon became soft, and began to dissolve and digest. On viewing the villous membrane before applying the bread crumbs, the mucous coat and subjacent follicles only, could be observed; but immediately afterwards, small, sharp papillae, and minute lucid points, situated in the interstices of, and less than, the mucous follicles, became visible; from which exuded a clear, transparent liquor. It then began to run through the tube.

For the annals of medicine it was the first reliable information on gastric processes. Among the doctor's conclusions were these: that bulk as well as nutriment is necessary in the diet; that oily food is difficult to digest; that the time required to digest a meal is three to three and a half hours; that "stimulating condiments" are nonessential to a healthy stomach; that the constant use of "ardent spirits" produces disease of the stomach; that hunger distends the vessels that secrete the gastric juice; and that the quantity of food taken at a meal is often larger than needed.

The results of these experiments were recorded in his classic book, *Experiments and Observations on the Gastric Juice and the Physiology of Digestion,* published in the United States in 1833 and thereafter in England, France, and Germany.

The second Fort Crawford Military Hospital was restored in 1934 as a memorial to Beaumont. It is today a registered National Historic Landmark and is operated as the Museum of Medical Progress and Stovall Hall of Health, owned and operated by the Charitable, Educational and Scientific Foundation of the State Medical Society of Wisconsin. In the reconstructed hospital are exhibits depicting the Indian medicine man, the military fort physician, the family doctor then and now, great events in the development of surgery, and furnishings of physicians' offices of 1850 and 1900. It is a splendid place in which to look back over the years that have passed since Beaumont conducted his experiments.

In due course, by the time of the War Between the States, Fort Crawford was abandoned, for it had served its purpose. But in few other places did so many things happen over so long a period as at Prairie du Chien, and in few places does the spirit of the frontier linger so warmly.

For the last hundred years, Prairie du Chien has remained one of those towns with rare good fortune and insight: It has not eliminated the evidence of its past.

The town has done the best it could to recall the memories of those early years, and to preserve the physical vestiges of an era significant in national history. For total recall, there is much to be done; it might be possible to reconstruct a great deal of the town on its original site, a kind of Williamsburg on the Mississippi. If so, there could hardly be a handsomer start than the Villa

Louis, an enchanting window to the past. Through the Villa Louis we may enter immediately an era when canoes loaded down with furs were among the most impressive signs of progress.

In earlier days, Prairie du Chien was oriented more to the British community at Mackinac than to anywhere else because traffic moved along the northern shore of Lake Michigan, up the Fox River, and down the Wisconsin.

That made Prairie du Chien a junction of north-south traffic on the Mississippi as well as east-west travel on the Wisconsin.

It was in Mackinac that Hercules Louis Dousman was born, first of seven children in a militia officer's family. It now seems apparent that his herculean capacity for work, as well as an astuteness in business, manifested themselves while Dousman was still young, and caught the eye of John Jacob Astor, for whose American Fur Company Dousman worked six years in Mackinac.

Astor sent Dousman to Prairie du Chien in 1826 as his confidential agent, and from then on the fur trade, bustling already, burgeoned. Dousman dealt not only with Indians and traders, but with governors, generals, explorers, and others of eminence who passed his way.

It was a rough-and-tumble businessman's community, and the only way to bridge all of its disparate human elements successfully was to be fearless, fair, and honest. Dousman obviously was all of these, as well as smart; his position led him to power, wealth, and extraordinary respect.

The house he built in Prairie du Chien became a showplace on the river frontier. When the army gave up the site of Forts Shelby and Crawford because they were too subject to flood to permit expansion, Dousman bought it. His purchase was not a bad bargain because an Indian mound set back from the river a few hundred yards rose high enough to avoid the floods and had room enough to accommodate his house and office and appurtenant structures.

Here he built what was for those times an almost palatial mansion, a virtual castle in the wild. He called it, as any bachelor prosaically might, the "House on the Mound." When he married in 1844, his wife, Jane, a relative of President Monroe and a member of a distinguished French family, changed its name to "Le Château Brillant."

That was the beginning of an elegant era in Prairie du Chien—of carriages drawing up to the door, of satined ladies and silk-hatted men, of generals whose swords were sheathed in gold and jewels, of steamship lines, horse races—and all at the edge of the frontier wilderness.

For nearly 25 years the Dousmans lived there, and after he died in 1868 his wife lived on, remodeling the house and adding to its artistic treasures.

Today it is called the Villa Louis and has changed very little from the era when the Dousmans occupied it. In 1935 the heirs gave it to posterity; it is owned and operated by the State Historical Society of Wisconsin and is a registered National Historic Landmark.

As we walk across the grounds or stroll through the graceful halls, we may envision the lively times that transpired here. The laughter can almost be heard in the drawing room, which, with its chandelier of Waterford glass crystal, is as elegant as when the family lived here. In the corner sits a Steinway concert grand piano; it is silent now, but its notes must have been a memorable experience when this was the far frontier.

From the library come, in our imagination, the voices of the men—traders, freighters, merchants—telling of current affairs in Mackinac or Saint Louis, or the changing mood of the Indians. They sit in chairs of rosewood covered with tufted red satin; behind them is a marble fireplace; at the side are tilt-top tables inlaid with mother-of-pearl. Their feet rest on a Belgian Aubusson carpet.

Dinners must have been on the order of royal banquets, with ornate silverware, hand-painted china, long-stemmed goblets, and steaming dishes of venison or wild fowl brought in from the kitchen. An icehouse on the premises was supplied each winter with 15 to 20 tons of ice from the Mississippi, which usually freezes over at this place to a depth of three feet; this provided not only refrigeration in summer but, through a system of pipes and ducts in the mansion, a primitive form of air conditioning.

Such ingenuity is not altogether unexpected on the frontier. What is unusual is to find a spot where so much of the original has been preserved for 130 years.

Now the sounds of finches and pewees fill the air; where once the children of pioneer days shouted on the greensward and their voices echoed in the dell of the Mississippi a few steps away, the laughter of living children is mixed with the roar of motorboats and passing trucks.

Yet the past is still here, singing out to be understood and enjoyed: the blockhouse of the first Fort Crawford; the Villa Louis, with its laundry, icehouse, dairy, preserve room, carriage house, and ponds with great willows sweeping over them. In this spot one's mind expands to all the frontier. For the frontier is collected here, in nuance and boldness, in delicacy and coarseness, in the remoteness yet relevance to what we are and what we do today.

The Villa Louis is open from spring through fall. A great many people are indeed charmed by it, because the number of visitors is rapidly approaching 100,000 a year. How does each of these visitors, engulfed in the mansion, bridge the gap of time encompassing a century or more? As though he had entered a time machine, he is suddenly a part of the Dousman family, a part of the fur empire. There is no Space Age as he knows it, but rather a space of land beyond the Mississippi that flows at his feet, a territory as unknown as the moon.

Many sounds come to him in the silence of the walls of this mansion—music, laughter, business, sadness, even prayer. Upstairs a chapel was installed, complete with altar, statue, font, benches, and banks of candles.

The whole house is an extraordinary museum in itself, with a treasure of Victorian furnishings—urns of Italian bronze, samplers, portraits, velvet drapes, a French Boulle clock, marble statues, a stained-glass window made in Italy.

Walnut bookcases are jammed with elegant volumes of the period: the ninth edition of the *Encyclopaedia Britannica,* Butler's *Lives of the Saints, Great Painters of Christendom, L'Art, La Sainte Bible,* Audubon's *Birds of America,* and Martin Luther's *Table Talk* of 1567, printed on the original Gutenberg Press.

Madame Dousman's "morning room" contains a piano and melodeon, sewing machine, walnut furniture upholstered with horsehair, and, as if she had just gone away and left them there, copies of *Godey's Lady's Book,* which show all the latest fashions of 1850.

Upstairs the bedrooms are furnished with such period pieces as a sleigh-bed, canopy bedstead, and a marble-backed washstand of rosewood. The bedrooms still contain lace bedspreads. A wardrobe in the hall holds sumptuous gowns worn here. Toys in the nursery were used by the Dousman children.

A great deal of the official business of the family was transacted across the outer stone walk in a separate building. Here was Dousman's office, and today it looks about the same as it did when he and his assistants made their plans, kept their records, and wrote in their ledgers. An oil lamp sits by the window. On the desks are blotters and plume pens. Dousman's books of the fur trade are still in this room. So are his cap, rifle, cane, bootjack, drinking water kegs, safe, letter-press, Ben Franklin stove, and other accouterments of the era.

A reality and presence about this office puts you squarely in the headquarters of the high command of the fur trade. You feel a personal link with the traders out on the frontier or those coming down the river in fur-filled canoes. For a few brief moments your forward progress is reversed; you are released from the present and carried back in time to a place where you can be whatever you wish—*voyageur,* fur trader, soldier, settler, surgeon . . . .

Outside passes each form of transportation as the years go by: birch-bark canoes, pirogues, keelboats, rafts, steamboats. All called at Prairie du Chien. In 1857, when the railroad arrived, the bulk of commerce changed from river to rail.

And if it's a humorous experience you want you can imagine how it must have been to stand beside a bearded and eccentric young Scot named John Muir and try out an iceboat. Fresh from demonstrations of his inventive abilities at a Madison, Wisconsin, fair, Muir arrived in 1860 to help test another inventor's answer to winter travel on the Mississippi—a flat-bottomed, steam-powered boat designed to carry both freight and passengers across the ice.

When finally tested, the contraption collapsed too often to go anywhere or carry anything. But that was nothing to stop John Muir. While waiting, he did odd jobs around Prairie du Chien and entered into the social life of the time, though later he looked back on himself there as an uncouth youth.

After the iceboat fiasco he went back to Madison and enrolled at the University of Wisconsin, where his fame as an inventor of clocks and other objects made him popular. But his enduring fame was not to be as an inventor of clocks but of words and ideas in the natural world. He would become what some persons regard as a great conservationist, a father of national parks and forests.

In some ways, we all have the spirit of adventure that these men had—their curiosity, their enthusiasm, their humor. We may not make use of these attributes in quite the same way, but they are there. And lest our spirits sag, or we abandon the will to wonder and laugh, it is good to submerge ourselves now and then into the lives of the frontiersmen.

It is fortunate, therefore, that Prairie du Chien has stabilized a few of its priceless epochs in physical, visible, enjoyable form.

The United Nations has cited tourism as the largest single item of world trade, which means that we may be gradually replacing some of the extractive and consumptive industries, perhaps even halting the once-glamorous developer who tears out the old to put in the new.

Man may, in fact, be evolving from reflex animal conquests to a rational examination and intelligent use of the resources he has, both old and new.

All it takes sometimes is imagination. The assets of the past are here in good order—the Villa Louis, Fort Crawford, the military hospital, Effigy Mounds. And because they are, we can enjoy the one great secret of this outpost on the Mississippi: History is alive and well at Prairie du Chien.

Natchez Trace 🦅
Tennessee·Alabama·Mississippi

MORGON STUND HAR GULD I MUN.

Layer on layer of oak leaves shut out most of the commencing light. But as dawn came, the sun climbed slowly from leaf to leaf, turning each gold, so that we seemed to be enveloped within a cocoon of mottled gold and green.

The morning hour had gold in its mouth—the old Swedish saying was never more true.

A thrasher awoke and flew among the blueberry bushes and patches of sumac. From a hidden perch, but seeming to issue from everywhere, the song of a thrush floated through the forest.

Dogwoods had already bloomed, as had the redbuds, earlier carriers of the message of spring. Now the leaves wore a fresh chartreuse, and some a scarlet from new growth, adding a distinctive color for this time of year.

Thus came morning to the woods of western Tennessee. It was tempting to linger, but we had a great deal to do, and with only ten days to travel this historic southern route we had to get on the move.

Packing up our camping gear, we drove through golden shafts of sunlight and shadowed, leafy avenues around a circular road that climbed a hill. The way led to an old gray cabin that stood in an open swale.

Birds sang in concert. A woodchuck ambled out of sight as we arrived.

Over at the side of the clearing, we saw an old abandoned roadway curving into the woods. You could not drive a car along that road, nor possibly even ride a horse through the brush that had grown up over it. Just walking would be difficult enough.

But it could be done, even though a hiker would have a hard time trying to find his way northeast to Nashville, 70 miles away. Parts of the route have been obliterated in the century and a half since anyone used it, and the same is true in the other direction. On the opposite side of the clearing the road disappears among thick oak trunks on its way southwest to Natchez, nearly 400 miles away.

In Indian days the route was little more than a trace, in places only a random coalescence of wildlife trails. It passed through lands of the Choctaw and the Chickasaw, and in a time when no superhighways connected villages, it came to be an important trace, whether vague or not.

The more the Indians used it, the more clearly defined it became, and when the first Europeans arrived, it at least was a recognizable route through the wilderness. The British called it the Path to the Choctaw Nation. Others called it the Chickasaw Trace. From both ends, Natchez—a frontier post on the Mississippi River—and Nashville, it led to the Indian villages near where Tupelo, Mississippi, now stands. In time it took on the name by which history remembers it: the Natchez Trace.

From 1760 on the traffic increased, and as we stood there at the edge of the glade that morning, watching the path disappear into the woods, we could almost hear the hoofbeats of horses carrying traders, preachers, soldiers, settlers, bandits, boatmen—

Yes, boatmen. The early "Kaintucks" used to load their local products or their produce onto rafts in the Ohio River Valley, float downstream to New Orleans, sell both merchandise and raft, and go home by way of the Natchez Trace.

How they must have cursed as they covered their heads with cloth to ward off clouds of mosquitoes, or strained to free their wagons from the muck of rivers and swamps.

For the most part, though, the Natchez Trace was built on ridges, a high road being far less wet, less hot, less densely vegetated.

Just the same, it was often a nightmare, something rather hard to tolerate, considering how well traveled it became. The capital of Mississippi Territory, dusty, squalid Natchez, was about as isolated from the rest of the country as any place could be. This, too, had become intolerable; the brewing of war—with Spain, with France, with Britain, with Indians—made clear to Thomas Jefferson that this route must be transformed from trace to highway in the shortest possible time. He ordered the military to improve it.

Thereafter, troops marched down the trace when war threatened in New Orleans in 1803 and when it finally came in 1812. Over this path Andrew Jackson led the Tennessee Militia to Natchez and back again, sharing the hardships with his men, and gaining the nickname of "Old Hickory." At its peak, this route was used by as many as 10,000 travelers a year, many of whom moved along in groups for security against marauding bandits.

Except for birds, the trace is more or less quiet today. No hoofbeats of horses or curses of wagoners rend the silence. In some ways the peaceful woods are as lonesome now as they must have been then. We appreciate the solitude today, but the riders of that era must have had their fill of loneliness and wilderness after 500 miles of oak and sweetgum and catbrier.

Among the men who went along this road were some whose names are still well known. A private secretary to the president, for example, had just led an expedition from the mouth of the Missouri River to the mouth of the Columbia and returned. He was Meriwether Lewis and, assisted by William Clark, he had obtained the first extensive knowledge of the territory west of the Mississippi River.

Afterward Lewis became governor of Louisiana and, in 1809, at 35 years of age, started a long journey to Washington. He intended to travel by ship, but near what is now Memphis he changed his mind and took the Natchez Trace.

On October 11 he reached the forested glade in which we stood. What happened that tragic night will never be fully known. An inn, composed of two cabins, occupied the glade at that time, and Lewis took a room for the night. But all was not well. He was upset and angered. He felt harassed. He was disgusted with politics, the unsympathetic attitude of a new president, and his own tangled fiscal affairs.

He must have been brooding all the way, for he paced the floor, talked to himself, smoked, went outside. Sometime after midnight two shots rang out through the clearing. Accounts of events the rest of the night are confused or incomplete. The following morning Meriwether Lewis died.

He now lies buried in the clearing, and a monument rises above his remains. We felt a certain awe in being so close to the man who led the first exploration of the Northwest, and not a little surprised to find his remains where he finally fell, on the Natchez Trace.

We also thought of Andrew Jackson's army on the triumphant return from the battlefields of New Orleans in 1815.

But all men, even the great, are temporary, and the events of their times only fleeting moments of adventure. The Natchez Trace itself became historic with the advent of steamboats, which eventually carried traffic to and from New Orleans. After that, parts of the trace were abandoned and parts used as local roads.

Though the men and their times are gone, the trace remains in pieces here and there and has been memorialized by construction of a federal parkway, the Natchez Trace Parkway, that follows the original route fairly closely.

The sun climbed above the leaves. The gold disappeared. We moved on, out to the Natchez Trace Parkway, and headed south on a road that was far better engineered than the old one, with gentle curves and open vistas of the Tennessee woods and hills. No billboards. No traffic signals. No commercial traffic. We could not have had a better introduction to the South.

We did not get very far without coming to another point of interest. There we turned off and descended into the bottomlands where the Natchez Trace crossed the Buffalo River.

The woods were full of the sound of mountain water. Once they echoed with the sounds of ironmaking, for from the Napier Mine, a few miles to the south, came enough ore between the 1820s and 1920s to keep a smelting furnace humming.

Ironmasters, gunsmiths, millers, tanners—craftsmen had been the crest of the second wave of settlement, men who came to serve the original frontier families and make life tolerable in an untamed land.

All that remains of Steele's Iron Works is part of a shallow ditch that once brought water to the furnace. But the Buffalo River itself now attracts a great deal of interest. For over a hundred miles from here to its mouth it affords good floating, and if you think there is no wildness and adventure left in these Tennessee hills, just set a canoe on the Buffalo River.

There are hazards aplenty. Capsizing is common because of hidden shoals or snags. The nests of hornets hang low over the water, and anyone brushing the limbs from which they are suspended may learn an enduring lesson.

These lowlands are home for water moccasins and snapping turtles. Even where the trace crosses the river one may see the heads of numerous reptiles when they swim through the water probing for prey along the banks. In the woods are copperheads and timber and pygmy rattlesnakes.

Yet the trip has a certain majestic beauty, a lure of bass and bream and catfish, a reassuring quiet, and such stimulating memories as that of a wilderness camp at the river's edge. And all this despite the fact that hardy adventurers come from many states to make the trip, some groups bringing as many as 18 canoes.

Moving on down the parkway we reflect on the greatest significance of the region today—its natural environment. We are surrounded by nature. The Natchez Trace has always been surrounded by nature—the dominant feature of the trail and the major influence on travelers along it.

As a sign on the parkway says, "This early venture in interstate road building produced little more than a snake-infested, mosquito-beset, robber-haunted, Indian-pestered passageway through the forest. The pious lamented it. The impious cussed it. All found it a trial of strength and patience."

Torrential rains and floods balked and bogged down travelers. Riders had to unload their horses and swim the animals across, then, with luck, find a fallen log upon which they themselves could cross.

"I passed through the most horrid swamps I had ever seen," said the well-known, well-traveled naturalist Alexander Wilson. "These are covered with a prodigious growth of canes, and high woods . . . which shut out almost the whole light of day for miles."

Horseflies, gnats, ticks, chiggers, and mosquitoes plagued each passerby, and so did thieves, who sometimes sneaked away with horses.

Not all of these problems are as persistent as they were back then. The modern parkway was authorized by Congress in 1938 and when completed will be

NATCHEZ TRACE PARKWAY, TENNESSEE-ALABAMA-MISSISSIPPI:
top–Mississippi Ferguson's Mount Locust Inn;
left–magnolia; *bottom*–bark of persimmon tree,
near parkway's Sweetwater Branch;
right, top–Springfield, mansion near Mount Locust;
right, bottom–split rail fence
along Old Natchez Trace at Mount Locust

a continuous strip of ride-awhile, stop-awhile road 445 miles between Nashville and Natchez. It has been under construction for more than 30 years (appropriations come slowly) and presently consists of 5 disconnected sections measuring from 6 to 165 miles in length. Acquisition of land is not a federal expense; all lands or rights-of-way are acquired and conveyed to the United States by the three states through which the parkway passes.

Even though unfinished, there is enough of the route open to help us go back to a good many yesterdays while at the same time capturing the grandeur of the present. If we hurry, the route can be covered in a day or so, but the Natchez Trace Parkway is not intended for hurriers. By poking along, by being inquisitive, by using an artist's mind and eye, we can discover what others miss. Detect, reflect, reveal—there are hundreds of pockets along this path in which we can lose ourselves. Which shall we choose from all that become available during the day?

The uplands. We turn off to the left and drive for a mile or so along a reconstructed portion of the original trace. The forest is at rest and at peace; if we have been hammered at from time to time, and our sanity has suffered, here is the place to restore it.

The views! Between some boles of oak we see a vale spread out several hundred feet below. Are those turkeys down there? They might be quail. It is too far to see. The softness of the greenery veils our sense of size and distance. A cabin stands at the edge of fields just sprouting with corn. Faintly the voices of chickens come to our ears, but they are no match for the songs of vireos over our heads.

Surrounding the vale and clothing the high horizon is a thick-set mat of trees, the leaves and branches so dense that we cannot see to the ground at any point among them. Around us, behind us, above us stands a similar upland forest of oak and hickory.

Time gets away. We go on. We stop. We cross the Tennessee River and pause for a swim and a picnic. The images come rapidly and furiously: a flash of red and black as a summer tanager flies across a meadow; crows rising from the road and moving off through the trees; a pair of woodchucks wandering away; groundsels, daisies, phlox, and fire pink at the roadside; butterflies, cardinals, blue jays, bluebirds, quail—

We are witness to more than we can see, much less attempt to understand.

The song of the bobwhite, clear and piercing, issues from the side of the road, a musical score for the setting sun. The light of day goes out. Stars and fire-flies appear as we cross into Alabama. We stop and listen and are suddenly startled by the loud, high, rapid notes—sustained and changeless—of a chuck-will's-widow, southern cousin of the whippoorwill.

Thirty to forty times a minute the phrase is repeated, with such resolution we think it will never end. All else in the woods seems asleep or suspended; the sound has a special quality of penetration and travels through the forest with ease where other sounds are absorbed. A bird with a voice like that can afford to be reticent and retiring; its music is the music of the universe.

The next day found us wandering in the lowlands along a crystal stream. In the openings we were assailed by the fragrance of honeysuckle and all about us were its pink and white and yellow blossoms smothering the trees.

Past river birch, within the fold of the forest, our path was strewn with pastel orange petals from tulip trees. May apples graced the shadows, often in masses and frequently associated with banks of ferns.

If the natural succession of plants in such lowlands were to continue, un-disturbed by fire, tempest, disease, or man, the mixed hardwoods might be replaced in time by oaks and hickories, with water-loving species holding on in swamps.

But such a succession succeeds only rarely, if ever, and something is always going on in these woods. A giant beech tree, cracked, aged, half gone, looking as though nothing could hold it up much longer, overhangs the stream. Some day a gust of wind will push it over; with that the stored-up nutrients will return to the soil so that other generations of life may grow.

Black walnut, one of the most handsome native trees, grows in these low-land forests. We duck under hanging grapevines. Our faces are brushed with spider webs. We see the tracks of animals, and hear in the hushed surroundings the inter-mittent rustle of leaves and the vanishing sound of footsteps.

For a long while we stop and examine the bark of persimmon, broken into nearly symmetrical plates and patterned in a way that distinguishes it from other trunks. While thus engaged we see a wraithlike insect, giant though slender, per-haps three inches long, with a long proboscis thrust for another three inches into a hole in the tree.

We cannot begin to tell what it is. Evidence suggests that the deep, narrow hole has been horizontally drilled by this organism. Yet the creature is so wirelike and fragile that we wonder how it could bore so deeply into wood so hard.

Its motions are slow and deliberate. It is not frightened by our presence and perhaps does not even see or sense us. There is obviously only one object in its life, but what? Will it deposit eggs within this cavity? We have some research to do when we get back home. Time denied our wish at that moment: to remain beside this creature and see what it was doing, what it fed on, what fed on it.

We had to drive on, and as we did, swallowed in a seminatural environment, we tried to think of life in the years before modern man—life without stores, without mail-order catalogs, without guidebooks to the wilderness.

First were the prehistoric Indians; evidence exists of thousands of years of human occupation in this region: camps, villages, fortifications, heaps of shells, burial places, and mounds. Bynum and Emerald mounds are found adjacent to the parkway and readily accessible from it. Emerald Mound, one of many earthen ceremonial structures in the Mississippi Valley, is 35 feet high and covers an area equivalent to five football fields. It is the third largest mound in the United States and it was built between A.D. 1300 and 1600 to support temples and ceremonial structures.

The Indians themselves, ancestors of such groups as the Natchez, Creek, and Choctaw, were religious and obviously devoted to their labors. They led the complex lives of farmers, craftsmen, hunters, and gatherers, and if a traveler along the parkway wonders how the Indians—ancient and not so ancient—lived, he can stop and visit the site of a former Chickasaw village.

At that point once stood a fort and several circular houses with plastered walls. These are gone, as are the Chickasaw who built them, but, as always, nature has survived. In the woods adjacent, a trail has been designed and constructed to show how human beings made a living from nature's bounty.

It is only an introduction, this roadside herbal, but it lives and renews itself each year and gives us specific insight into the lives and times of the Chickasaw, their brethren, and their ancestors.

Some things they pulled right off the tree and ate, such as persimmon, although if they picked it too soon, before it was ripe, it would "draw a man's mouth awry with torment."

Logs of juniper turned into walls for their homes; the bark was used for roofs; the heated, wetted twigs provided a cure for headache. Indians pounded sturdy strands of red mulberry with which to manufacture rope, cloth, and hair-nets; extracted an oil from hickory nuts for cooking; brewed the leaves of cherry for tea; smoked the leaves of sumac; dropped the ground-up poisonous seeds of red buckeye into streams to stupefy fish; hollowed out the trunks of black tupelo to fashion drums.

Dyes they had in plenty, including yellow from sassafras, orange from su-mac, black from walnut. They ate the shoots of greenbrier as we do asparagus, and collected the roots, which were chopped and dried, ground up, combined with corn-meal, fried in bear grease, and offered as fritters.

Medicines for all ills were dispensed by the forest. Extracts from the devil's walkingstick, or Hercules'-club, cured toothache (or perhaps only stemmed the pain for a while). An oil of swamp chestnut oak was kept in gourds for anointing the heads and joints of patients or ritual participants. Black cherry wine was a pain-killer. As a standard remedy for snake and insect bite, members of war parties carried a chunk of root from the button snakeroot; if and when he was bitten, a warrior chewed the root and applied it to the wound.

Gum, or balsam, must have been a medical favorite, for the Indians used it to conquer a good many internal ills, as well as to heal their wounds and "gladden the heart." And in spring they drank sassafras tea to "thin the blood."

And if at times of important powwows they wanted to sharpen their wits (or lose them, depending on how you look at it), they concocted a black intoxicat-ing drink from the berries and leaves of yaupon, a species of holly.

By the time a hiker has finished this trail of food and medicine he is willing to believe that, with all the animal life available, the Indians got on rather well.

Incoming settlers also lived off the land, finding some of the Indian products palatable, and adapting others to their own desires, tastes, and needs. Two other labeled side trails on the parkway, one at the Tupelo Visitor Center and the other at Jeff Busby Park, divulge the lot of the frontiersman, which was not altogether a bleak existence.

What was better than flexible, good-splitting white oak wood, for example, for barrels, baskets, and shingles? The settlers, like the Indians, had food just for the plucking every season: plums to mix with venison and bear fat, acorns to grind into flour, pawpaws to eat or fill pies with, mulberry fruits, beech and hickory nuts, eatin' greens, and wild grapes.

The settlers seasoned their meats with hickory smoke, their brandy with black cherry. Out of the flowers and pods of redbud came delicious fritters. And there were hawthorn jelly, chestnut soup, sumac lemonade, honey, holly tea, and beechnut "coffee."

From the elm came rope to tie their bales of cotton; from juniper the fragrant wood for "cedar" chests; from willow the charcoal for gunpowder. Black cherry was in such demand for furniture that rough-cut lumber was hauled away to Natchez and New Orleans.

Unfortunately, the woods were so depleted that none of the mature original forest remains along the 450 miles of the parkway, and the present forest will not grow back to its original dimensions for another two centuries.

In any case, the pioneer settlers are gone, and their techniques and ways of life have almost disappeared.

Wandering through these woods and getting glimpses of the past, we lose all sense of time. Our passage down the parkway becomes a series of objects, images, thoughts, places, events, all interlocked and blended.

Witch dances; Hurricane Creek Trail; Red Dog Road; beaver dams; the Black Belt of rich prairie soil; wars between the English and French, between the French and Chickasaw, between the North and South (Tupelo, Brice's Cross Roads); Tockshish, a relay station where post riders exchanged weary horses for fresh ones; early Christian missions; a military road; the Choctaw Boundary; the Treaty of Dancing Rabbit; Chickasaw Indian Agency; the Indians surrender, are forced to give up their land; the Indians go to Oklahoma.

Pigeon Roost Creek and the millions of migrating passenger pigeons that used to be; Jackson, the capital of Mississippi; chickasaw plum; sunflowers; opossums; voices of frogs in wild ponds; red-tailed hawks; indigo buntings; the pointed leaves of sweetgum, most important hardwood tree in southern forests; place names: Pellaphalia and Chuquatonchee creeks.

Even this is only a modest listing of what there is to discover. Each stop takes several minutes, or an hour, or a day to absorb and to reflect on, and sometimes even a day is not enough. We find to our dismay that the week and a half we thought would be ample for this trip will not be enough at all.

Then suddenly we see the first absolute proof that we have entered the heart of the South: an oak festooned with Spanish moss. In the gentle breeze these trailing threads swing back and forth, and flow out on the air like fragile tresses. The plant is not a moss but rather a member of the pineapple family; it is also epiphytic, attached to other plants but not parasitic. Curtain after curtain, tuft on tuft, it adds a special grace to southern lowland flora.

A short time after, beyond the point where the Pearl River lures us to a picnic at water's edge, we are on foot again, descending an old abandoned river channel into one of the most unusual environments along the Natchez Trace.

Huge trees with enormously swollen, buttressed trunks grow directly from the swamp. They are bald cypress, a member of the pine family that sheds its leaves each fall (becoming "bald"), and water tupelo, a member of the sour gum family.

The rounded buttresses of these trees provide an otherworldly appearance, as do the cypress "knees," the hollow, knoblike root growths that extend above the water like little sculptured totems.

Dark shadows, somber reflections, silence—all give this swamp a menacing mood at first. But the more we remain, the more we see its fascination: the jungle effect of giant cane, the process of life renewal as shown by plant-covered logs, the modest grace of dogwood. From high overhead the yellow green light of fresh spring leaves filters down, and it seems as though a hundred chandeliers have been suspended among the uppermost limbs.

On our way again, we pass a park ranger and are reminded that the Natchez Trace Parkway is a unit of the national heritage, under vigilance for the benefit and enjoyment of future generations.

Even though it is a recreational resource, no effort has been spared to see that the parkway is developed properly, that connections to the past are sustained with dignity, and that there is much to see, do, and be inspired by.

Appropriations have always been modest, which perhaps is just as well, for it allows facilities to be installed with prudence and with painstaking care; so far the primary roads along the parkway constitute a $66 million investment that rises in value every year. One hundred miles of the parkway remain to be

154

constructed, and it is hard to foretell when the job will be finished. Nearly all land has been acquired and deeded to the federal government, but construction funds are allotted by Congress in accordance with the exigencies of the times.

There are some 10 million visitors along the parkway annually, a large part presently commuter traffic in the absence of parallel interstate routes in Mississippi.

Trucks, praise be, are eliminated.

Inevitably, however, administering such a strung-out unit of land is not an easy job, and people bring problems. Law enforcement is involved primarily with moving traffic violations; some 2,000 citations for speeding are given each year. Added to this are two or three dozen cases of driving while intoxicated, 200 motor vehicle accidents, 65 fires, a couple of dozen requests for rangers to assist in road blocks, 50 cases of major crimes, 70 incidents of destruction of government property, plus vandalism, poaching, and timber trespass.

Traditionally, wilderness animals of the region belonged to the settlers; now times are changing, and shooting along the parkway is strictly prohibited.

So is drag racing, but rangers have had to set night traps to stop that practice. Wildcat whiskey is made in the area, and one raid by state authorities netted 22 stills; parkway rangers, however, do not usually participate in this aspect of law enforcement unless, of course, the stills are constructed on parkway property.

It takes about $1.25 million per year to maintain and protect the parkway, which calls for a substantial staff to insure the investment. There are 3,000 neighbors along the route, some of whom require a disproportionate amount of official attention, because of minor encroachments, political requests, and spiritual overenthusiasm.

By and large, however, the neighbors are friendly, the parkway is pleasant, and opportunities for carefree enjoyment are abundant. In addition to markers, museums, trails, and points of interest, there are special weekend programs given by rangers in the campgrounds during summer.

Hundreds of camp and picnic sites are planned along the parkway, and many now exist. Someday it might be possible to hike the length of the original Natchez Trace, as a few persons already claim to have done, and some day it may be possible to establish bicycle trails along or near the parkway.

Down through the country of the Chickasaw and Choctaw, deep into Mississippi, we near the end of the journey. Along the way are sites of early stands, or inns:

> John Gregg, at the lower Choctaw line, respectfully informs the public, and travelers particularly, that he keeps constantly on hand a large supply of GROCERIES, ground Coffee, ready to put up, Sugar Biscuit, Cheese, Dried Beef, or Bacon and every other article necessary for the accommodation of travelers going through the Nation, on very reasonable terms. He is also prepared to shoe horses on the shortest notice.

We read of Mississippi Ferguson—merchant, farmer, innkeeper, magistrate, sheriff—and visit his inn, Mount Locust, one of the oldest structures in Mississippi (circa 1780). Mount Locust has been restored as nearly as possible to its condition as a frontier home of the 1820s when it catered to travelers on the old Natchez Trace. Sometimes these travelers had to sleep in the loft or on the floor, with saddles for pillows.

As we walk around the inn, perched on a hill overlooking a vale with attractive split rail fences, we marvel at the giant stumps of sassafras logs that constitute foundation pilings. They are original, we are told, and thus must be amazingly impervious to insects and decay.

Mount Locust is one of the finest places on the parkway to obtain a glimpse of the more primitive past. As for elegance, we need not look far away. When the mansion Springfield is restored, one will be able to walk along its veranda and look out over the level fields and majestic oaks—as perhaps Andrew Jackson and Rachel did, for it is believed that they were married here.

The vegetation becomes more distinctly southern: bayberry, American hornbeam, water oak, with always the fragrance of honeysuckle.

Then we arrive at a place long awaited, and stop for a walk along one of the roadbeds of the original trace, a fragment more than three miles long, now unused and adorned with tassels of Spanish moss. The earth in this region, a soft and sandy loess, is easily eroded, and during years of trampling by human feet or horses' hooves, and the rolling of wagon wheels, the trace was cut to depths of 18 feet.

156

Walking in the bottom of such a cut, with the curving and coiling roots of trees on either side, we seem to be in a shadowed gully from which a frock-coated bandit will spring at any moment. The trees lock their limbs overhead so that all is gray or green above instead of blue. The sun penetrates in a few places only and picks out trailing nets of Spanish moss to spotlight in the gloom. There is no sky, no horizon; only an open-air dungeon, if such a thing is possible.

In this quiet vale, which nature is taking back again, there is a silence and serenity unmatched on the parkway. You are miles from the noise of modern machines and years from the troubles of the present. You pass through spider webs you failed to see, and now and then reach down to flick off ticks that crawl up parts of your outer clothing.

When the rains fall or the plants encroach, the old trace washes and withers away some more, and its era of history sinks a little further into oblivion. In the distance, faintly, we hear the whisper of a jet going over. Then again there is silence. At times in this shadowed depression not even a bird may sing.

And then, at last, there is Natchez. This city is famous for its mansions and probably has more elegant homes per capita than any other. They would have disappeared decades ago, decaying and crumbling, if the citizens had not bestirred themselves. As it is, the mansions bring back a part of that opulent era when Natchez was the capital city.

Built as plantation homes to a large degree, some nearly 200 years ago, they amount to a priceless collection of classical antebellum architecture and furnishings. Shaded by live oaks and magnolias, their walks are lined with azaleas, camellias, crepe myrtle—and memories.

Some have names that reflect the natural beauty of the region—Twin Oaks, The Elms, Green Leaves, Fair Oaks, Mistletoe, Holly Hedges—and their halls resound with historic names and events, conspiracies, feuds, and "romantic traditions."

Natchez was, after all, a center of wealth and aristocracy in the Old South. Here lived Varina Howell, whom Jefferson Davis took for a bride and married at The Briars, on Natchez Bluff. Here Aaron Burr was tried for treason. Here Davy Crockett and Jim Bowie spent some time. Here General Grant stayed when Union forces occupied Natchez.

The mansions are showpieces, and income from an annual pilgrimage—

when some 30 homes are opened and hostesses in hoopskirts offer their hospitality—helps to keep them refurbished.

Walk into Rosalie, for example, a house of home-burned red brick near the edge of the bluff overlooking the Mississippi River, and the world of the old romantic Natchez is remote no longer. This is where Bienville, the French governor, established the first fort on the Mississippi and named it "Rosalie" for the Duchess of Pontchartrain. The United States flag was raised here for the first time on Mississippi soil.

As you wander through the double parlor, into the dining room, upstairs to the bedroom where Grant slept, you see the glorious trappings of the time: French crystal chandeliers, hand-carved rosewood furniture, a piano with keys of mother-of-pearl and gold-plated strings, and salmon-rose satin damask hangings and upholstery. The banquet table is of mahogany, with silver service, Sèvres china, and a white Wedgwood pitcher made to commemorate the coronation of Queen Victoria in 1837.

So superbly have generations of Natchez residents kept their homes intact that it is almost as though time had stopped about 1800. That very fact, that feeling, is the essence of this place, an able assist to anyone's imagining himself back in the time of the old trace.

And, of course, there was always the hustle at the docks beneath the bluff, where paddle-wheelers tied up, perhaps where the Kaintucks had their last wild fling with civilization before taking off homeward up the long route of the Natchez Trace.

At length the time came for us to depart from Natchez, and we had the choice of returning home some other way. But we were drawn again to this old "path of empire" as a theatergoer returns often to see some great drama that never grows old.

In the air of honeysuckle we were almost mesmerized while we drove back up the parkway that evening. With the setting of the sun, soft mists began to rise imperceptibly from the fields and marshes.

Once again the landscape turned to a green and gold. As the sun had risen leaf by leaf that morning more than a week ago, it descended now from layer to layer of leaves, and burst at times through an opening in the woods, like a bucket of molten gold pouring forth.

In a while the gilded beams came almost horizontally through the little openings, spotlighting a patch of grass or a trunk of hickory or the white plume of a thistle. In time the sun became a golden disk and finally disappeared.

When it had gone and darkness had settled over the land, the music of the wilderness reaffirmed that nature would endure. As if to prove it, the call of a chuck-will's-widow suddenly sounded from a thicket at the edge of the woods.

🌿 The EAST

THE HUMAN ECOLOGIST, WHO DEALS IN ULTIMATES, HAS A professional interest in if, when, and where the final series of crises for man will begin (or whether it has begun already) and what the results will be. If nature intends for man to march like lemmings and springboks to the sea when his numbers become too many, the human ecologist would like to know how many is too many.

Men may not march to the sea, but if there is to be a first big test of overpollution and overpopulation, where will it be?

East of the Appalachians, some say, in the seaboard megalopolis. But there are still a good many places in the East where one may retire now and then from the pace of an urban environment or, with 5,000 miles of continent in which to expand, depart altogether.

Then perhaps there is a populous island, heavily industrialized, where man's only choice might ultimately be, indeed, to march to the sea. This description, from what we had heard, seemed to apply to Puerto Rico more than anywhere else. So, curious, we went to see, and found some unexpected surprises.

Which brings up a crucial question. If the environment is finally cleaned up, will we be ready for it? Will we know how to use it the second time around?

The number of secret places in the East is immense: hidden hammocks in the tropics and subtropics; mangrove swamps with roseate spoonbills; hard-to-get-to lakes with rare wild flamingos; a shallow bight where once in a while a crocodile comes to the surface; the sea islands of Georgia; Okefenokee Swamp and the Suwannee River; crystal streams like the Cacapon in the mountains of West Virginia; Cape May and the Pine Barrens of New Jersey; Sunfish Pond in the ridge and valley country. . . .

To many persons, New England, with its mosquitoes of summer and persistent ice of winter, is simply to be avoided. After all, it lies astride the parallel of 45° north, halfway to the North Pole. The map itself is convincing evidence: Human settlement becomes more sparse as one goes north.

But conversely, the numbers of moose and caribou increase.

Thoreau deplored the leaping of men away from lands of the East to seek spectacular discoveries toward the West. He knew that there was more in this region than any human being could discover and enjoy.

It took us a day to find our way to Little Wilson Falls and back in the wilderness of Maine. It took that long because we got lost going and coming—wanted to get lost, and did, and enjoyed it—and because we stopped so often to rake raspberries from bushes along the trail. That day has lived and been relived in memory.

Among the kames and kettles of Cape Cod, in the forest beyond the moors and bogs, there is a special hidden lake of bright translucent blue. Much of the East has peace and quiet as in Deans Ravine, Connecticut, and wilderness such as that along the Allagash Waterway, Maine.

An outsider might mispronounce a few of the names: Chemquasabamticook Lake, for example, or Isle au Haut. But that does not matter. You could travel a dozen well-known rivers, yet none might have the personal impact of a simple unnamed stream, a secret place you care about and love perhaps without any reason above the joy of loving. It is a piece of the earth that you have come to understand a little more than others.

Such connections—man and earth—ought to occur rather often, it seems, and such adventures ought to be repeated because of the biological link that holds us to the land, the forests, the waters, and the energy of the sun, from all of which we came. Of these commodities, the East has an abundance.

By far the best way to know them is to get out on the Appalachian Trail, which threads the peaks of the Great Smoky Mountains, the Blue Ridge, the Green Mountains, the White Mountains, and the Maine woods, linking them into one continuous, joyous entity. Tough going it is. Stairs is often a better word than trail. The route leads through marsh and swamp and over the bold rock outcrops of tree-less mountain peaks. The trail goes only where rugged men and women have wished it to go, and this means over and around some difficult terrain. The trail demands that you get out of your car and onto your feet, under a pack and away from your cares.

Nothing that we know better takes us back to the original American land-scape, northeast or southeast, than the wilder portions of the Appalachian Trail. Nothing introduces us to so many hidden places as a walk somewhere along this 2,000-mile footpath. So for those easterners who fail to find surcease of sorrow near their own accommodations, it is likely to be but a few hours' drive to a place of access on the trail, or at least to a trail in some national, state, or local park.

From there, you are on your own. The places that nobody, or almost no-body, knows wait only to be discovered. And what grand discoveries they are!

El Yunque, Puerto Rico 🍃

MOUNTAIN MISTS CAME SWEEPING UP AND OVER THE BAR-
ren peak, enveloping us in a swirling white fog. For a few moments the clouds, with
a trace of tropical fragrance, played about the summit, then as rapidly as they had
blotted out the view they blew away.

All Puerto Rico lay at our feet, vividly green, lined with yellow sands along
the beaches, bordered with wave-white rims and an emerald green that gave way to
the deep blue of the distant sea and the light blue of the tropical sky.

We stood almost transfixed, as if about to be engulfed in the great green,
blue, and white phenomenon that spread from here atop El Yunque all the way
down to the sea, nearly 3,500 feet below.

On the right, a forest of sierra palm perched on the sunlit slopes. On the
left, a storm tumbled across the mountains, its dark clouds falling down and raking
the ridges with claws of rain.

All creation seemed to be in motion—the wind, the clouds, the storm, the
colors, the shadows, the sprinklings of light, the strands of moss that clung to the
trees but unfurled and flapped like so many flags.

Far below, quite evidently, the landscape was much less pristine. Houses,

houses, houses dotted the hills and vales. Patches of dull brownish gray sediment flowed from the coastal streams and merged with emerald waters along the shore. Far to the west lay the glittering glass and steel of sprawling San Juan, almost hidden by haze.

On the day we had flown into San Juan we wondered whether the island's nearly 3 million inhabitants, who must crowd onto little more than 3,000 square miles of land, were faring as poorly as we had heard. The people had choked their island with industry, we had been told, and all that was left was theft, corruption, slick hotels, casinos, and petrochemical plants.

Puerto Ricans themselves had told us that they were progressing from an agricultural economy to a burned-out land of disaster more rapidly than any place on the mainland because they had no place to expand, nowhere to ship their wastes, no place to hide from the final effects of overurbanization—not even in the sea.

It sounded like just the place to pass by. Go on to Trinidad and Tobago, the seasoned travelers had warned, or Grenada, where beauty remains and thrives; in Puerto Rico there is not much *rico* left.

We were almost persuaded. Our first impression of San Juan had been: Miami all over again. Another Honolulu. Another Mar del Plata. Another—

But we kept on with the hope that somewhere the original *Puertorriqueño* character must have endured. Somewhere there must be enshrined the original homes, the forts, the music, sculpture, architecture. And somewhere there must be remnants of land, wild land, which the Latins refer to as *belleza natural*.

We fled as soon as we could—from the glass and concrete hotels, the beaches that workmen raked and swept each morning before the bodies rolled out on them like carpets of reddish flesh, the polluted lagoons, the acrid smoke, and the streets of grinding traffic—and went into Old San Juan.

What an exchange of environments!

On a cliff at the edge of the sea sat the famed Castillo de San Felipe del Morro, thrusting out a rocky fist that dared an enemy to approach its battlements or come within range of its cannons. Puerto Rico had been a final bastion of Spain in the Antilles, for the surrounding islands had fallen to the British, the French, and the Dutch. Had the fortress of El Morro not been there, guarding the entrance to San Juan Harbor, the island might have succumbed much earlier. As it was, the old city knew sacking, plundering, siege, and burning at the hands of enemies.

Yet when the smoke had blown away on the warm sea winds, there stood El Morro, as always, proud and impregnable, one of the most powerful strongholds in the Americas.

The fortress was bombarded during the Spanish-American War in 1898, and United States forces later landed on the southern coast, but an armistice was reached, and that same year the defenses of San Juan were turned over peacefully to the United States. With El Morro intact today, and administered by the National Park Service as the San Juan National Historic Site, the conflicts of the colonial Caribbean remain alive, and anyone may climb its ramps, "fire" its cannons, explore its inner passageways, and see from its abutments the sea and the city and the mountains beyond.

From there we went on down into Old San Juan, back into the world of early Spain. At the time of Columbus's arrival in 1493, Puerto Rico was a frontier between the peaceful Taino tribes of the Greater Antilles and the fierce Carib tribes of the Lesser Antilles. Conquest and colonization were initiated in 1508 by Don Juan Ponce de León, who became the first governor of Puerto Rico. Since then the islands have seen turbulent times: gold rushes, pirate attacks, wars, and industrial expansion.

Yet in Old San Juan remain a few of the more charming aspects of yesterday's lives and times: the colorful courtyards, narrow streets, elaborate balconies, gardens, plazas, patios, fountains, and chapels with silver altars.

As we stood atop El Yunque, the avenues of Old San Juan seemed far away in time and spirit. Here, immersed in clouds and fresh, pure air, with the grand *belleza* below, we knew that we were as close to the real Puerto Rico as men could get. If we could erase the roads and fields and houses, we could almost conjure a picture of the island as it was when Columbus came and when Ponce de León and his men explored its riches.

Puerto Rico is about 100 miles long and 35 miles wide. Up here, surrounded by forest, we found it a little hard to remember that nearly 3 million people lived on the island and had built 6,000 miles of roads.

Puerto Ricans have been citizens of the United States since 1917, and the island has functioned as a "commonwealth" and an "associated free state" in alliance with the United States. The islanders have their own constitution and bill of rights, but are associated with the United States in such matters as defense, diplomacy, postal service, education, roads, and public health.

We had talked at considerable length with Luis M. Juarbe and Otto Reyes those first few days. At that time these men were members of the Department of Tourism, an important segment of Puerto Rican government because more than a million visitors come from overseas each year and leave behind some $200 million. In an era when manufacturing and agriculture were primary industries, Luis and Otto and others had begun to question whether the island was simply a rock on which to set casinos and refineries regardless of the consequences, or whether it was one on which to care for priceless native forests and restore in them the voices of vanishing birds. This kind of thought was almost heretical in view of Puerto Rico's published offer of 26 inducements, including tax incentives, designed to lure industrial developers.

One day Luis took us in his plane for an eight-hour aerial introduction to the island: up over El Morro and south beyond Barranquitas to the deep defile of the Río Usabón; northeast over Luquillo Beach; a long loop around El Yunque; above the multiple islands in a deep blue sea off the eastern coast; in and out among the ridges of the Sierra de Cayey; and a landing for lunch on the semiarid, mangrove-studded coast near Salinas.

We took off again and flew to islands far offshore, then circled back to Ponce, second largest city on the island. Just beyond lay a tangle of pipes and storage tanks, with leaping flames releasing long black plumes of smoke, that signified one of the island's vaunted industrial plants. Smoke and fumes rose into the air on dependable trade winds, blew across the southwest quarter of the island, and turned the once-clear tropical sky into a dull gray haze.

Flying at 2,000 feet we entered the smoke and got a splendid whiff of the scents combined of benzine, olefin, alcohol, paraxylene, and nitrogen. Coleridge would have counted more than "two-and-seventy stenches" here.

Following the southern desert coast we swooped down over La Parguera and the famous Phosphorescent Bay, and then to the extreme southwestern corner of the island, where salt flats gleamed in contrast to the turquoise waters offshore; finally we turned north and flew above palm-studded beaches past Boquerón. Our second landing was at Mayagüez, the university city on the western coast.

Late in the afternoon we found ourselves above the enormously pocked and pitted uplands between Bayaney and Sabana Hoyos. Puerto Rico abounds in geologic phenomena that are almost classical. Its Karst topography, for example, is superb. A Karst region is one of limestone marked by such holes as sinks and caverns that have been dissolved by water. The Karst region of Yugoslavia is a classic example; the Mammoth Cave region of Kentucky is another. Puerto Rico possesses scores of rounded buttes and giant mounds that are clothed as much as the cliffs allow by a rich vegetation. There are so many natural sinks that it looks as if the island had been bombed in an all-out war, or been struck by asteroid fragments. One of the sinks has been turned into a radar and radio wave reflecting bowl for the Ionospheric Observatory, whose instruments probe the universe.

The land is also broken into canyons, dissolved similarly by water, and hollow with caves that contain stalactites and stalagmites. Nothing is stable. The tropical forest holds fast where it clings to the land, but everything is subject to constant change, even though this change may seem very slow to human eyes. At times, however, the alterations are rapid; owing to its position in an active seismic belt, Puerto Rico shifts and yields at times to earthquakes.

We landed late that evening, mentally endowed with an enormous collection of Puerto Rican vistas in many forms and shapes and colors.

The next day we drove away from San Juan for a closer look at secret places. West of Aibonito the road rose into the mountains, and we were soon enclosed by the vigorous tropical forest. A few impressive flamboyán trees still held their bright red petals, though these were falling and coating the roads with scarlet. In other places the roble, or Tabebuia, trees let fall their delicate pink corollas in a colorful carpet that would be almost as temporary as the winds.

We stopped in Toro Negro Forest for a picnic lunch accompanied by sounds of falling water and the music of birds. Then, dropping down from the central cordillera, we drove through Ponce and west to Guayanilla. The arid cactus country was magnificent, and for a while the air was bright and clear. Then we came to the petrochemical plants over which we had flown the day before. Odors infiltrated the car and stayed with us for miles downwind.

Relief came as we reached the forest at Guánica. The contrast could not have been more absolute. Not only was the air much fresher, but here, unlike the wet rain forests, the lands lay covered with desert flora. Two species of

EL YUNQUE, PUERTO RICO:
left–Calle de Cristo, Old San Juan, Puerto Rico;
middle–*Coqui* frog of Puerto Rico;
right–fronds of giant tree fern in rain forest,
Caribbean National Forest;
bottom–palmate leaves of Cecropia tree

cactus, both of tree dimensions, were prominent in this ecosystem. One had stout columnar branches like the Cereus of Arizona; the other was a prickly pear that stood ten feet above our heads and bore red flowers along the edges of flattish pads. Most common trees on the dry hillsides were the red-barked almácigos, known in Florida and Central America as gumbo-limbos.

That night, off La Parguera, we went out in a boat with Dr. Máximo Cerame-Vivas, director of marine sciences at the University of Puerto Rico's College of Agriculture and Mechanical Arts at Mayagüez. Heading east we left behind the lights of the village and were soon enveloped in blackness.

Suddenly, small green lights appeared on the surface of the sea. Palolo worms, Dr. Cerame-Vivas guessed; they were shedding luminescent gametes and possibly eggs, a rare phenomenon in these waters.

Many organisms around the world emit such biological luminescence, some in more than one color. The process is a chemical one involved with the release of energy from living cells, and is markedly related to daily cycles of light as well as to the rhythms of evolutionary progression.

A few moments later we entered Phosphorescent Bay itself, which contains one of the world's greatest concentrations of luminescent life. In the narrow entrance to the bay the wake of the boat began to glow as millions of dinoflagellates (*Pyrodinium bahamense*), each about 1/500 of an inch in diameter, emitted tiny flashes of light on being disturbed.

The luminescence of such free-floating organisms is commonly seen at the cutwater and sides of moving ocean vessels, but in a few coastal bays conditions of salinity, depth, and contour are conducive to special concentrations of them. Puerto Rico has been gifted with three outstanding luminescent bays, none more than 14 feet in depth.

We moved into the bay through a density of perhaps 700,000 dinoflagellates per gallon of water. The sea around us began to glow. The boat became a silhouette against a soft blue submarine light.

Fish darted out of the way, their paths through flashing organisms resembling meteor trails, some straight, some curved, some swerving wildly.

We stopped. The bay became dark again. We stamped our feet on the deck and a score of fish departed in all directions, leaving their meteoric light trails.

We reached over the edge and scooped up handfuls of flashing water, then filled a bucket and poured it back into the bay, watching the luminous splash. When rowboats came into the bay, we were told, the oars dripped with light as boatmen paddled across the surface. Swimmers splashed in a sea of "fire." And one of the most spectacular displays occurs when rain patters down and turns the surface into multiple bursts of silvery blue.

It is without doubt one of the most unusual and spectacular natural displays in the Western Hemisphere. On the way back, Dr. Cerame-Vivas explained that seawater entering the bay sustains the delicate ecosystem of which the dino-flagellates are a part. He deplored the entry of oils, chemicals, and other residue from cities and industrial plants to the east, impelled by easterly winds and currents. He felt that at the present rate of pollution the bright display might last no more than another 25 years.

That the bays are in danger was authenticated in a report completed by a team of National Park Service specialists who made a critical study of the bays and surroundings. "The bioluminescent bays are delicate and fragile systems," they wrote. "They depend upon an input of organic material that is partly offset by an exchange of water with the adjacent sea. Only a certain ratio of input to exchange is capable of supporting bioluminescent displays, and the rarity of such bays throughout the world testifies to the extremely narrow range of this ratio. . . .

"One of the most crucial factors in the well-being of these bays is the maintenance of the manner and rate with which their water exchanges with that of the outside sea. Each bay has a particular flushing rate that balances the organic input from its mangrove fringe to provide the nutrient 'broth' capable of sustaining a high population of *Pyrodinium*. Should this ratio of water exchange be altered, the bioluminescence will disappear."

The report cites a similar bay in the Bahamas, which was dredged to permit large boats to enter the bay. The bioluminescence disappeared and still has not returned.

A number of problems arise from this delicate situation. The report expresses concern about the multiplication of resort homes in the La Parguera area. These are often houseboats or dock-type houses built over the water. Without sewage treatment facilities in the village, an increasing volume of raw refuse is released into the sea. This alters not only the ecological balance of the mangrove waterways adjacent to La Parguera, but also that of the coral reefs which parallel the shore for several miles to seaward.

We had now seen enough to know that the charm of the original Puerto Rico still existed—but had to be looked for. Coming back to San Juan, we met with Governor Luis A. Ferré and told him how impressed we had been with Phosphorescent Bay and of our concern for its future. He described the desire of his administration to clean up the surroundings that contribute pollutants to it.

Ferré is a dedicated humanist and conservationist, and can hardly help being something of a historian; he is the 150th governor to occupy La Fortaleza, the oldest executive mansion in the Western Hemisphere. As he took us on a tour of the walled fortress, with its imposing circular towers and handsome patios, there was no denying that here was the stuff of which the real Puerto Rico was made, and that Puerto Ricans were already conserving the crucial parts of their cultural heritage.

No better manifestation of this could be found than the Institute of Puerto Rican Culture. The more we saw of its work, the more we were determined to talk with Ricardo Alegría, its director, and did so later that day at his handsome restored home in Old San Juan.

He was quiet and unassuming, but his contribution has been one of the most significant to Puerto Rico in decades. The institute, an agency of the island government, had been created by the legislature in 1955 as a public corporation to preserve and enrich all aspects of music, ballet, theater, literature, folklore, art, and history. It has restored more than a hundred historic structures in Old San Juan, and is working on a hundred more. Tax incentives and other inducements encourage cooperation on the part of private landowners.

The institute, which has as its purpose "to preserve the cultural character of the Puerto Rican people," has sponsored the preparation of a series of phonograph records of early compositions and folk dances in popular and contemporary styles.

It also cares for ruins around the island, of Dominican churches, forts, and famous houses as well as of pre-Columbian antiquities. Near Utuado, in the central uplands, lies the site of what was apparently the most important ceremonial center of Taino Indian culture in the Antilles. Around a central plaza are ten rectangular but lesser plazas and one that was circular in shape. Now excavated, the principal plaza is lined with granite monuments, some as tall as a man and weighing more than a ton. It is a source of wonder how the primitive architects hauled these from a riverbed a hundred yards away. There are petroglyphs on many of the monoliths, and nearby are old stone paths that pique our curiosity.

All this shows the excellent progress made by *Puertorriqueños* in the field of history and culture. We discussed with Governor Ferré the need for parallel efforts for the *belleza natural,* and efforts were underway. Luis M. Juarbe was later appointed to the natural areas program, and is assessing the island's remaining resources. If he has his way, a great deal of the original natural Puerto Rico will be saved. The public is supporting him, and the press has begun to observe some of the traumatic effects of locating industries in the wrong places. Conservation foundations and natural history societies have been formed and are helping to spread a common awareness of the situation.

All this has come about rather rapidly. Three decades ago Puerto Rico existed in a rural economy from which it lifted itself into affluence through an economic program known as Operation Bootstrap. Since the first major industrial plant, a glass factory, was opened in 1945, the number of plants has risen to some 3,000.

For years there have been complaints about soot from sugar mills; now public pressure is rising for the industries to clean up or close up. At a meeting near Guánica, whose historic bay has been filled with a nine-foot-thick accumulation of sludge from nearby industrial plants, citizens pleaded to government executives: "Take it away. We don't want any more industry if this is what it is going to do to us."

Early in 1970 a group of 150 Guánica fishermen filed a damage suit in Federal District Court asking for $3.5 million from two chemical companies and an insurance firm. They charged the defendant corporations with deposit of industrial wastes and toxic substances that killed marine life and ruined the fishing industry. Yet at that moment new petrochemical plants were under construction, and the government had before it a commercial proposal to dig an open-pit copper mine near the central ridge of the island.

"Puerto Rico needs industry," answered a legislator whom we asked about this, "and it must be dispersed to places where the people are. Some persons are against these mines but we have to strike a balance. I am trying to see that the environment is protected, too."

We asked about residue from the pits.

"There will be tailings," he admitted. "It is a low grade ore, less than one percent copper. We'll have to take out a great deal of rock, but the companies assure us that it will be economically feasible."

And where would be put the thousands of tons of tailings that would accumulate each day?

"Oh, we have that solved. We'll take them out to sea."

An article some years ago, called "Puerto Rico Swallows the Hook," maintained that Puerto Rico had taken the lure of quick industrial profits and was hell-bent on destroying its image of an island paradise. Only a few people, the article said, understood the consequences of exploitative, extractive, at-any-cost development. That number has been rising, and since 1960 the proponents of environmental awareness have been growing more vocal. As one writer in the *San Juan Star* said in early 1970: "Let us make peace with nature today, mañana may be too late."

There are other signs. The birth rate may well be declining, perhaps the result of natural biological revulsion to overpopulation. There have been predictions that the population will stabilize in time; such a situation may come about only far in the future, but it will be quite an accomplishment in a land where the average rural housewife used to bear seven children in her lifetime.

Many parts of Puerto Rico have, at one time or another, been recommended for protection: reefs, hot springs, virgin forests, scenic canyons, mountain ranges, swamps, beaches, and a few of the offshore islands. Thanks to foresight on the part of the federal and state forest services, some 80,000 acres of naturally attractive backcountry have been set aside from public lands or purchased from private owners, demarcated, protected from encroachment, reforested, and developed with roads, trails, and recreation facilities.

As mists swirled over the top of El Yunque, the stir and commotion of "progress" seemed remote. The rainstorm had cut over the ridge and gone to the southern side of the mountain. Clouds to the south had risen and opened, letting in the sun to reflect its rays off the glistening slopes.

The misty atmosphere gave the scene an almost veiled appearance, as though a screen of fine lace had been drawn across it. The sun was beginning to descend in the west; a few of the roofs in San Juan glinted in the distance.

It was time to move on, for another evening's *coqui* chorus would soon begin. The *coqui* is an audacious frog that has almost become a Puerto Rican mascot, praised in word and song and even in the gold of jewelers' creations. A dozen or so kinds of *coqui* exist, and the genus is found elsewhere in the Caribbean. The common Puerto Rican species produces a distinctive, inquisitive "ko-KEE? ko-KEE?" by which it gets its name.

The *coquís* of El Yunque seem larger and paler than others, but they are still not very large, scarcely an inch in length. For that reason, and because their world is one of shelter among the leaves and secluded tree trunks of town or forest, they are seldom seen. To hear them is common; the note of the *coqui* is very probably the most widely heard and recognized animal sound in all of Puerto Rico.

With the coming of twilight their inquiring calls begin, sometimes extended to a "ko-ko-KEE-KEE-KEE?"

By dark the individual sounds have blended into a chorus that rises in crescendo, coming in waves that seem to echo up one forested ravine and down another. An hour later, and for the rest of the night, the hundreds of notes, mixed with the music of insects, become almost a solid roar. If a night rain pours into the forest—which can sound as though it were falling in barrels instead of merely in buckets—the roar is moderated, but afterwards *coquís* come back stronger, louder, and seemingly more excited than ever.

The human ear, unaccustomed to being so assailed, wearies eventually, yet there is a fascination in the sound and we become captive to it, trying to distinguish the notes of individual frogs and to find a thread in the music where there is no thread. In due course we become used to the noise and hardly record it consciously—something that seemed unlikely at first.

By the time the light of dawn filters among the sierra palms, the *coqui* chorus has become reduced to the notes of a few individuals. With the coming of the sun they quiet down, withdrawing into the axils of leaves and yielding their domination. For the rest of the day they are silent, or nearly so, and we long to hear them again.

In this supersaturated forest the rainfall reaches up to 200 inches a year, which contrasts with a low of 5 inches a year on the southern coast of the island. Because of such a variation, some 4,000 species of plants grow wild in Puerto Rico, including 100 kinds of orchids and 500 species of trees. At least one of the tree species is believed to reach an age in excess of 3,000 years.

A giant of the forest is the ausubo, which was used in days gone by to make the great beams that still support historic structures in Old San Juan and El Morro. Near one of the many waterfalls we came to a balsa tree, lightest of commercial woods (it weighs less than cork), whose giant, heart-shaped leaves shone green and white in the sunlight as the winds twisted them around. The deeper shadows were illuminated by bursts of red, the flower clusters of African tulip trees, an imported species.

The central public recreational portion of the Caribbean National Forest is accessible by paved highway and receives nearly a million visitors a year. Yet sometimes a special perception is needed to appreciate so luxuriant and complex an ecosystem. We stood one day near the highway observing and photographing giant ferns. Tabonuco trees towered into the sky, lianas fell away to the ground, and banks of ferns covered 40-foot slopes nearby. While we were admiring this scene, a car stopped and a passenger said: "We're looking for the rain forest. Can you tell us where it is?"

In some ways this rich forest is a final refuge for nature. The Puerto Rican parrot, for example, used to inhabit most of the island, but with the coming of men, and the animals they brought, the bird has diminished. As late as 1957 a census of 200 parrots was made; now the number is well under 50.

It was a special pleasure, therefore, to hear their squawking cries pierce the leafy canopy and to see a flock of five sail over on rapid wingbeats. But enemies make their lives precarious. Much of their former habitat around the island has been replaced with fields of cane and pasture grasses. The rat, an imported enemy, scampers up and down the trees at will, feasting on parrot eggs and young. Another imported enemy, the pearly-eyed thrasher, of which thousands live in this forest, destroys the parrots' nests and then usurps the site.

There are also cats, mongooses, and tree boas, and one wonders how the species has lasted so long. At this writing a team of ornithologists is attempting to learn key features of the birds' life habits, out of which a crash survival program may arise.

Yunque is the Spanish word for anvil, the shape of the upper peaks of the mountain range when seen from a distance. However, the name of the best-known peak may also have originated in the Indian word *yuké,* "white land," which referred to the clouds that often cover the summits.

The mountains have had a history of protection from the time when they were preserved by the Spanish crown in the 1870s to their present status as part of the Caribbean National Forest.

On our hike to the top so many secrets unfolded we could hardly keep track of them. A night shower had cleansed the air and freshened the foliage, and we set out in the cool morning air at a temperature of 74 degrees.

Sierra palms made star-shaped designs overhead, the sunlight shining through their leaves and turning green. Bromeliads festooned the palms like graceful decorations, some yellow, some green, some deep red or with orange and yellow flowering stalks, some so thickly clustered we could hardly see the trunk of the tree. There were also orchids, small and often unnoticed until approached more closely, but elegant in their flowers that ranged from white to maroon.

Straight overhead the palmate leaves of the yagrumo hembra, or Cecropia, a member of the mulberry family, flew like multiple flags above all else. The leaves collected in clusters measuring as much as 40 inches in diameter.

The high-pitched squeak of banana quits sounded frequently. Now and then a quail dove cooed or a parrot called. A few *coquis* succeeded in posing their familiar question, but only weakly. Insects buzzed. And there were frequent sprinklings of water down tiny cascades beside the trail.

We walked among galleries of rocks that were padded with ferns, moss, lichens, and liverworts. Our boots rustled through discarded Cecropia leaves, white on one side and brown on the other.

En route to the top of El Yunque we passed through four distinctive but sometimes overlapping associations: rain forest, montane thicket, palm forest, dwarf forest. At the start, the canopy was almost solid; every opening was taken, all spaces were occupied. Beneath were only tunnels and shady vales where light came in as pinpoints of sun that managed to make their way through the layers of leaves.

It was a soft, well-cushioned world, insulated from extremes of temperature, cool and wet and nearly quiet.

Masters of this extensive flora were the tabonucos and ausubos which, with thick, straight trunks, pushed their crowns of leaves up through the roof of the woods to the sky, a hundred feet or more above. The tabonuco, described by botanists as the most majestic tree in Puerto Rico, has always been in demand—by settlers as a source of resin for calking boats, or of incense for religious ceremonies, or for making torches, and by modern men as a substitute for mahogany in furniture manufacture.

The roots and buttressed trunks of these forest giants make interesting studies in themselves, owing to their curving, rounded, massive designs of sculptural excellence. No two are alike.

All this is perhaps even more evident in the design and arrangement of the giant tree fern, whose growing fronds uncurl like the necks of violins; whose leaflets overlap in geometric mosaics; whose spore cases, seen against the sunlight, look like rows of platelets floating in a sea of green. At maximum height, the fern spreads out like a wide umbrella 20 feet above.

The trouble with so many trail phenomena was that we wanted to stop every dozen feet, turn around, and see what we had missed, or listen carefully to a distant sound. We needed time to survey and appreciate the changing views, to test the aromas, to explore in thickly vegetated ravines. But time was at a premium, since the day would be only 12 hours long. We began to believe, with such delightful delays, that we might not get to the top and back before dark. As a bullfinch whistled unseen back in the trees we hiked more rapidly up the trail, out of the true rain forest and into the montane thicket.

The changes in vegetation were subtle. Above 2,000 feet the trees became a little shorter and more gnarled. We passed through groves of sierra palm so thick that views of the lands below were seen only through tunnels of dangling leaves.

The way was not by any means lighted solely in hues of green. Begonias graced the forest floor, and even in shadowed places bore their cheerful flowers of white and pink.

Quite frequently, on rounding a bend in the trail, we came to a sudden, startling view of a yagrumo hembra tree whose leaves, backlighted, presented as brilliant a chartreuse as the forest offered. Twisting in the breeze, these leaves revealed their silvery undersides, and among the upper limbs grew an occasional rich green epiphyte with scarlet blossoms.

So much had now crowded into our consciousness that the views became less distinct, a montage of scenes and experiences, connected but disconnected, solitary but repeating, simple and clear yet somehow confusing.

It hardly seemed possible that 200 inches of rain fell here each year, for we had not felt a drop, and the trail was almost dry. Rains should have gouged out gullies to take away heavy runoff, but that was not necessary. Soil and rot and layers of leaves absorbed the waters almost as fast as they fell, and drained them away through subterranean channels to permanent springs and streams.

As we entered the upper forest, however, and reached the highest ridges, we saw the trees, much shorter than below, encumbered with hanging moss. In here were only breaths of breezes, but the upper parts of the forest were thoroughly pruned. Easterly gales must often whistle over these peaks. Combined with cooler temperature, this condition produced an environment less conducive to the kind of growth encountered in sheltered vales below. It was a true dwarf forest. The trail became a winding passage between the trunks of trees. Where sunlight penetrated, it flowed through fronds of ferns.

At last we reached the summit and took a side trail to El Yunque rock. The last steps were a clamber over cliffs, requiring handholds among the coiling roots and grips with fingertips in crevices of the rock.

Up over the edge we had come into the open air—or more correctly into the open passing clouds. We had arrived at the top of the world, where the green and gentle lands fell away below and where, beyond the slopes of palm to the east, lay the distant lumps of land that were Culebra, Vieques, and the Virgin Islands.

Having eaten and taken photographs, we repacked our haversacks and stood for one last look. No mortal man could reproduce that color, that drama of floating clouds and distant rain, or that great forest with all its life. Nor could any man re-create the simple succulent leaf of the guayabota which grew in the crevices of rock at our feet. At that moment we were prepared to believe, as the early Indians had, that El Yunque was where the god of good spirits lived.

Scrambling back down the cliff and over the root handholds we once again entered the precincts of enclosing forest, and by late afternoon we had gone down the southern spine of the range and had come to a viewpoint overlooking the eastern end of the island. Once more we paused to absorb the energy of forest and solitude on this tropical island, even though the last rays of light were fading fast, our path was growing dark, and the *coquis* were beginning to utter their nightly sounds.

Two white radar domes perched on a peak to the east.

We turned and surveyed the route we had just followed, and as our eyes moved along the ridge up to the top of El Yunque, we counted 59 radio and transmission towers.

Carry Ponds, Maine 🌿

T HEY WERE A WRETCHED LOT, STAGGERING FROM WEAK-
ness and hunger, covered with mud and ooze. They came out of the woods to the
edge of the pond and threw down their bateaux with grunts of pain and sighs of
relief.

All the way up the Kennebec River they had come, and that was bad
enough. The bateaux, alas, had been constructed of green wood. They were heavy
(400 pounds) and hard to row. They split easily and had begun to leak.

But things would be worse: leaving the river; climbing; carrying those
boats over gray rocks made slick by rain; packing provisions through the muck of
swamps . . . .

For the hundreds of ragged, bearded riflemen from Pennsylvania and Virginia it must have seemed like one "mire hole" after another. Thickets. Ravines.
Swamps. Precipices.

But now—these heaven-sent ponds! To set those clumsy boats on water, to
float again!

And so it was that these gentle lakes in the woods of Maine gave rest and respite to Benedict Arnold's tattered army, an army that fought not British here, but wilderness. The time: October 1775. The destination: Quebec.

There is not a hint today that such an army ever passed. We came to the edge of the East Carry Pond on a cool and clear October day nearly two centuries after Arnold and his men had passed by, but we saw no sight of their struggle. The birches wore yellow as they had that earlier October. The maples lifted leaves of crimson out of a forest gloom.

But we had no trouble calling to mind the scene as it must have been. If we used our imagination we might expect that at any moment Arnold could step out of the woods over yonder and ask for news of Daniel Morgan's men.

Under Ethan Allen, Arnold had earlier helped to take Fort Ticonderoga, but that had not brought full security to the ragged revolutionaries. Their flank to the north was open. If someone did not march to Canada, capture Quebec, and cut off British access to the colonies from the north, they might just as well return Ticonderoga.

Thus Arnold was in a hurry to capture Quebec. If he could do it at the beginning of the war, the strategic advantage would be tremendous. No matter the lateness of season: Speed was all that counted.

George Washington had seen in Benedict Arnold enough of the energy and daring needed to make him leader of the expedition. Moreover, Arnold knew the country; he had been through it frequently as a trader.

But now, advice on the chosen route turned out to be inaccurate as to distance and difficulty. Worse yet, the country was so thinly settled that it furnished a poor supply base for military operations of any size.

About the only advantage was that poor communications could help assure an element of surprise when the army finally got through and attacked Quebec. British defenses were reported to be somewhat in decay.

Arnold's force was composed entirely of volunteers: three companies of riflemen and two battalions of musketeers, a total of about 1,200 men. It was not enough, but Washington had counted on Canadians to espouse the cause and join the expedition as it passed.

So in mid-September 1775, more than 200 bateaux were built at the mouth of the Kennebec River—and the green flotilla headed north.

For a while the weather was good and, in the spirit of beginning a great adventure, the men did not seem to mind the force of the counter current, or even portages around waterfalls. They were tedious but tolerable.

Then the weather turned cold and the men's uniforms, constantly wet, froze on their backs. The hapless riflemen sat in icy water in the bateaux, or stood in it along the edge of the river. They slept in it during rain and flood. They watched it seep into casks of bread, swell them, break them, and sour the contents. They also watched it dampen and ruin the ammunition.

By the time they had been on their way a month, they were sick, exhausted, weak, and discouraged.

The locality listed in expedition records as "the twelve mile carrying place" involved four portages, including a three-mile climb from the Kennebec River to the East Carry Pond, then half a mile to a second pond, then nearly two miles to a larger pond.

"Either the front or the rear bearers were constantly tripping and falling, and the bateau sinking down and rising up," wrote Kenneth Roberts in *Arundel,* his fictional chronicle of the journey. "As we looked back at the line of bateaux crawling along this trail on the shoulders of their bearers it had the look of an ugly brown dragon painfully undulating between the high forest walls through which the axemen had hewn our path."

While the troops were struggling between these Carry Ponds, Arnold wrote many dispatches, some of which fell into the hands of Canadian officials.

Beyond the Carry Ponds the expedition ran into snow and bitter cold; the ration of food went down to a pint of flour each day per man, and then to nothing.

They ate whatever fish or moose they could find, but finally were reduced to consuming wood, bark, roots, dog stew, leather from shoes and breeches, string, snowshoe gut, and raw woodpeckers.

"The universal weakness of body that now prevailed over every man," one soldier wrote, "increased hourly on account of the total destitution of food; and the craggy mounds over which we had to pass, together with the snow and the cold penetrating through our deathlike frames, made our situation completely wretched, and nothing but death was wanting to finish our sufferings."

That came shortly: The final attack was a failure. It occurred on December

CARRY PONDS, MAINE:
left–maple leaf and star-shaped moss;
bottom–Moxie Pond
and 2,630-foot Moxie Bald Mountain;
far right–Shadow Pool,
near Shelburne, Vermont

31, 1775, and the Canadians, having learned of Arnold's intent, met the weary troops and killed a great many men. Arnold himself was wounded.

But failures may become as nobly enshrined as victories. This march now stands as one of the most grueling in the history of the United States.

Of 1,200 men who started to cross 800 miles of wilderness, 500 finally reached the Saint Lawrence River. Some had perished en route, while others turned back from illness, lack of provisions, or faintheartedness.

On our visit we had no boats to carry. We needed no ax to cut the way. We hiked the Appalachian Trail through golden autumn color around the Carry Ponds, and remembered an earlier time when we had hiked along the ponds in the summer.

The skin of our shoulders had not been scraped away by hauling bateaux over the mountains. We did not have to flounder to our armpits in the swamps. On a trail that was well maintained we seldom caught our feet in roots or rocks.

Today a hiker through these woods does not have to suffer pain and weakness, or have his legs gashed by jagged rocks or hidden stumps as the colonial riflemen did when they pushed their way through swamps and set their canoes into the water.

The only canoes now are those of fishermen. And if you stand at the edge of the pond long enough, you will see a beaver or two swimming out in the center, and these will approach in curiosity, if you move a bit, until they are scarcely a dozen feet away.

Otherwise there is quiet, and that great treasure of the forest, the fragrance of pine. But you can get a feeling of what those men went through who passed this way two centuries ago. The country they fought to establish still exists. The thick, rough forest in which they labored has gone, but a new one, perhaps with a little less pine, has taken its place.

Grass grows six feet high here and there. In summer, flocks of waxwings keep the trees abuzz with action, and the wail of the loon is heard now and then. In the autumn, squirrels nip off the cones of hemlock by dropping from one branch to another. Balsam fir trees, with their conspicuous pustules of sap, stand massively and quietly on the slopes.

At the edge of the Carry Ponds are shrubs, young trees, and marshy areas.

The cedar, a tree found in moist locations, grows at the water's edge in company with three maples—red, striped, and sugar—and on the forest floor are bunchberry, raspberry, moss, lichens, and numerous other species.

On this October day, for as far as the eye could see from the shores of the pond to every ridge beyond, there was a mass of yellow speckled with orange and red and spotted with clusters of conifers.

If the forest around the Carry Ponds was second growth, it lacked very little to dazzle the eye, and when we encountered a scarlet maple backlighted against the afternoon sun, it was as though we had suddenly come to a blazing forest fire.

Logging roads have been slashed through the woods from end to end, crisscrossing, zigzagging, intersecting. Some are so well grown over you can hardly find your way. Others are open, and you step only now and then through gently yielding bracken fern.

This gives the hiker or explorer access to the secret heart of the forest, and once there he casts off the mantles of sobriety and propriety and does whatever he desires to do.

Unlike the men of the Revolution, he comes to the woods to *smooth* it rather than *rough* it; he gets it rough enough at home, as Old Nessmuk used to say. Relations between men and forest have altered completely in 200 years. Arnold's troops came through the woods for war; men now come for peace and serenity, and for the change in environment frequently needed these days.

The hiker is free. He now possesses a garden of his own, a garden of maple and birch, with a wall-to-wall carpet of fern and moss. He stands in a chamber as open as the sky, air-conditioned as no other place is: with pure air scented with the essence of pine.

Everything he sees is his: his domain, his kingdom, his empire. He commands the trees and they obey. He orders the wind to do his bidding and it does. He summons the birds, the squirrels, the serpents. They are all there.

He becomes a part of the system. He does not fight or destroy it; he enjoys it. Every second he spends in this Elysium is a precious second in the eternity he never thought he would glimpse. Even five minutes here is enough to recharge his energies and rekindle the spirit he used to have and thought he had lost.

He wants to stay. He wants nothing to change. The golden leaves of maple seem to fill him with a golden glow as well. The warmth of red leaves of the sumac warms his soul. There is something private between him and the leaves, between him and the sun, between him and the sky and the laws of the universe.

No use trying to tell others what he feels here in his secret empire. They would not understand. From a distance they would not be able to sense the quiet, or fill their lungs with this air, or imagine just the proper, delicate shade of bronze he sees now in those leaves above his head.

Nor can he tell anyone how lighthearted he feels when the sinking sun compels him to draw away and start back down the trail. Lighthearted and full of laughter—he has not felt this way since swinging through those trees back home as a carefree child.

Having been assailed by cares through the years he had forgotten what it was like to be free, to let the mind wander and think up foolish things. He now knows better than before that life is too short to be wasted solely on cares. It was a good thought to take back: If you spend too much time making decisions, you never get any work done. If you worry too much about tomorrow, then tomorrow will not be worth worrying about.

At dusk the hiker returns to camp. The golden clouds in the heavens seem to have thrown up castles to confirm the celestial discovery, or rediscovery, he made today. Leaping plumes of cirrus, gilt-edged and glorious, rise above the castles toward the zenith. From the quiet, reflective surface of the Carry Pond, he receives a duplicate image.

And when he steps back out after twilight disappears, the stars look bigger than he ever remembered them. Overhead is Vega; over there is Coma Berenices; the Dipper is plunging toward the surface of the pond. His day has almost a cosmic ending. And why not?

As he leaves the Carry Ponds he knows them not only as landmarks on a historic route traveled 200 years ago but as a place where he found out once again that the world is a cheerful place and that its gladness and joy are his to command.

And so—here in the Maine woods you too may find a secret place of your own. You know you will return again if you can, to soak up the secret energy that exists here in unlimited supply. You will draw on that supply and take as much as you want without diminishing either its quality or quantity for someone else. Or you will find a forest nearer home, perhaps, and if that is not easy, you will rest content in knowing that somewhere the world holds beauty and perfection.

The universe cares for those golden maple leaves out there as much as for you. All life is part of that enormous, incredible, universal creation that no human being yet understands. You do not need to be above it; just to share it and be a part of the same great system is sufficient. It is a grand alliance.

*   *   *

The Appalachian Trail turns north from the last of the Carry Ponds, and less than 12 miles farther on reaches Pleasant Pond, where another famous figure in United States history had something to say.

Through the woods, across the Kennebec River, and up the valley of Pleasant Pond Stream, we follow the steps of a celebrated naturalist and essayist on outdoor subjects who came to this part of Maine in 1880 and seemed a little disappointed in what he saw.

"The traveler and camper-out in Maine, unless he penetrates its more northern portions, has less reason to remember it as a pine-tree State than a birch-tree State."

So wrote John Burroughs in "A Taste of Maine Birch." The white pine forests, he said, had melted away like so much snow in spring, but he found in the birch a fascinating subject for the study of woods lore.

Burroughs described some of that lore in his writings, such as the dozens of uses to which the bark of birch could be put. During a sudden shower his guide stripped off sheets of it to make umbrellas, and when the rain had ended, Burroughs wore the bark in front, like an apron, as defense against wet bushes.

On coming to a spring he drank from a birch-bark cup and vowed that water never tasted so sweet. He was convinced that butter, kept at camp in a birch box, improved in flavor. He ate oatmeal and maple syrup with a birch-bark spoon from a birch-bark bowl.

But the great triumph of this tree, said Burroughs, was the birch-bark canoe.

He saw one his guide had under construction that would hold five men. It had strong cedar ribs and spruce bindings and was sealed with pine pitch.

"What woodcraft it indicated," he wrote, "and what a wild, free life, sylvan life, it promised!"

John Burroughs cited other uses for birch bark—cabins shingled and sided with it, haystacks capped with it, plus napkins, tablecloths, paper, torches, fuel. One would think it highly durable, to have so many uses. Yet as a tree, the birch comes in on a temporary basis and does not remain very long in the forest. It yields preeminence ultimately to conifers, and when they shoulder it out and shade it, the birch succumbs and topples to the forest floor.

You can walk along a hill where spruce and hemlock have taken over and see in the shadows fallen trunks of birch that grew no doubt very tall and stately years ago. The logs look solid, but if you step on one, there is a puff of dust and it collapses beneath your weight. The inside has rotted away, leaving only the bark to hold the original shape.

"Our first glimpse of Maine waters," wrote Burroughs, "was Pleasant Pond, which we found by following a white, rapid musical stream from the Kennebec three miles back into the mountains."

Pleasant Pond Stream is still charming musically, but Pleasant Pond, a silvery clear lake in a mountain basin, has become adorned with summer cabins and NO TRESPASSING signs.

Burroughs said that the trout were veritable bars of silver until you cut their flesh, when they were the reddest of gold. "They appeared to be a species of lake trout peculiar to these waters," he wrote, "uniformly from ten to twelve inches in length. And these beautiful fish, at the time of our visit (last of August) at least, were to be taken only in deep water upon a hook baited with salt pork. And then you needed a letter of introduction to them. They were not to be tempted or cajoled by strangers. We did not succeed in raising a fish, although instructed how it was to be done, until one of the natives, a young and obliging farmer living hard by, came and lent his countenance to the enterprise. I sat in one end of the boat and he in the other, my pork was the same as his, and I manoeuvred it as directed, and yet those fish knew his hook from mine in sixty feet of water, and preferred it four times in five. Evidently they did not bite because they were hungry, but solely for old acquaintance' sake."

Seven miles through the woods from Pleasant Pond is what Burroughs called Moxie Lake, which he found to be an utterly delightful place, and where he lingered long appreciating the arts of fishing.

One day he hiked along the dim forest trail to Moxie Bald Mountain, past signs of caribou, deer, and bear, and to the summit, "the most impressive mountain-top I had ever seen, mainly, perhaps, because it was one enormous crown of nearly naked granite."

This raised in him some feelings of the eternity of time, and he noticed in the great cracks the tremendous power of ice expanding and thawing. There, too, were scratches and grooves of glaciers that had scraped over the mountain peaks, sheared them off, and smoothed down the landscape a little.

He saw nearly a dozen lakes and ponds. To the west lay Dead River, up which the men of Arnold's expedition had had such a terrible time transporting their boats when snow came upon them.

Nowadays we can enjoy the views with almost as much enthusiasm as Burroughs had. From Moxie Bald Mountain the alterations that men have made to Moxie Pond—the cottages lining the shore, the barrier and spillway at one end, the fluctuating shorelines, the morasses of destroyed vegetation, the stumps of old trees that have been flooded and killed, the boats upturned on the beach, and the crumbling docks—are obscured a bit by distance.

You can drive along the edge of the lake on an old railroad bed, and at the south end come to a point where the Appalachian Trail takes off into the woods. Pack on, boots clattering over the rocks of a stream or sinking into the soft earth of the luxuriant forest, you can take this trail and escape into the woods. You feel the freshness of the air. The path is hung with draperies of maple leaves, and here and there are outcrops of granite, a signature of the centuries.

Four and a half miles up the trail you leave the woods and step out onto the open granite, atop the world, reveling in the view that Burroughs had. In all directions, mountains rise from the multiple colors of the forest—the Barren-Chairback Range to the northeast; the knife ridge of Katahdin, 60 miles away;

194

Bigelow and Sugarloaf mountains to the west across the Carry Ponds; and the eminence of Mattamiscontis eastward toward Canada. The Kennebec River flows to the south. And over it all is the sky with a veil of haze, as well as the autumn wind, which ruffles the conifers and sings among their branches, goes to the golden leaves and lifts them from the limbs, carries them through the air for a while, and lets them fall to the forest floor.

As you traverse the yellow wilderness back to Moxie Pond, you can well understand why the Appalachian Trail Conference says that Moxie Bald Mountain is worth a day's exploration.

A man needs more than that if he is to explore and understand.

Quantico Creek, Virginia 🦋

THE NIGHT WAS WARM AND HUMID. AS WE CREPT THROUGH the swamp, the voices of frogs sounded idly from trees and pools, and the rasping of katydids scratched the silence.

No moonlight illuminated the way. Not even starlight managed to penetrate the multiple layers of oak and hickory leaves. We kept our flashlights pocketed, attempting to see in the barest of light where to place each step so as not to warn the wary beaver.

We had come upstream several days before, up Quantico Creek by daylight, along an easily traveled trail, had found the beaver dams and searched in vain for the occupants of the pond. Now, approaching from the other side, in dense, deciduous forest that lacked any trails, we hoped to see the beavers at a time when they were more active—under the cover of night.

Suddenly we discovered that we had lost our way, and could not tell in which direction lay the stream. We had come up over an embankment and out of the swamp, but now which way?

Disoriented, we stopped and tried to reestablish bearings in the blackness, and listened quietly in the hope of hearing some guiding noise.

196

Splash! Like a paddle hitting the water came the unmistakable sound. The beaver had announced its presence and given us an azimuth.

Cautiously we drew closer, trying not to be impatient and frighten the animal. All seemed well: from straight ahead came splashings and other noises that suggested business as usual.

At the edge of the pond, shielded partly by shrubs, we took up an observation post and watched a dark form moving on the surface of the water. It swam one way and then another, submerged, reappeared, submerged again.

After a few minutes we pulled out a flashlight and snapped it on. The sudden illumination startled us, like a lightning burst that blinds the eyes in a storm.

Everything sprang into form—the pond, the bank, the birches, the beaver. If the light caused us to blink it seemed to have little or no effect on the animal. Nothing in the beaver's evolutionary makeup had prepared it for brilliant light at night, so it made no move to swim away or slap its tail on the water and sink from sight. As we watched, it swam about its business, into the water and out, across to the other side of the pond and back, at times almost directly beneath the flashlight. Occasionally it turned its eyes toward the light, and we saw two tiny mirrors reflecting the illumination. But mostly there was only curiosity in these glances, and no apparent fear.

When we felt we had stayed enough, we attempted to sneak away without disruption of the beaver's life. But we must have made a careless step, or the beaver simply took routine precaution. Splash! Down went the tail, up went the water, and in went the beaver.

Our seance had ended. Evolution had endowed this animal with a wariness of movement along the bank, and to that it had responded immediately.

For a while, at least, we had touched the workings of the universe, and watched the wilderness progressing as it had, with few interruptions, for centuries.

The significance of this interlude was that such a piece of wilderness could still exist and its wildlife live in a natural way just a ten-minute drive from the suburbs of Washington, D.C. In a patch of recovering woods on Quantico Creek, adjacent to the Marine Corps schools, 11,000 acres have been set aside as a natural preserve called Prince William Forest Park. Once it was a recreation demonstration area, but is now administered by the National Park Service. In several ways it resembles some of the units of Chicago's Cook County Forest Preserves and is not unlike the "green necklace" or "green belt" type of sanctuary in such places as Cleveland and Cincinnati. All serve as splendid bases from which to launch inquisitive hiking trips and capture both the color and serenity of the woods.

Prince William Forest Park is located on the Atlantic Coastal Plain, which is covered by a lowland deciduous forest. A short distance outside the park Quantico Creek drains into the Potomac River.

During the 1600s tidewater Indians lived in this region. They fished, lived on forest plants and animals, and raised corn, squash, and beans. The following century brought European settlers who cleared the land and established corn and tobacco plantations. Tobacco was a leading export from Dumfries, the nearest village, then on the Potomac River and in its heyday second only to New York as an American port.

But with the lands cleared and topsoil loosened, floods brought sediment to the harbor and filled it. The port of Dumfries ceased to exist, and the village now lies inland.

Several Civil War skirmishes took place in 1862 near Dumfries and along the old Telegraph Road, a major supply line for the Union. In time the lands that had sheltered and served the Indians became so badly eroded and so infertile that they were nearly useless to the descendants of the European settlers. In the twentieth century the watershed of Quantico Creek was purchased by the federal government. The beavers, which had been exterminated in Virginia by the early 1900s, were reintroduced.

No matter what the season, the energies of this gentle wilderness wood have flowed into our veins. When snow falls into the forest a hush seems to settle over the whitened woods. We often follow the tracks of animals and search the surface of the snow for geometric circles drawn by twigs in the winter wind.

On snowless, blustery days, there are designs in the dancing trees. The flexible limbs bend across each other and nudge their neighbors beneath the fast-blown clouds, and for us there is an enormous exhilaration in hiking through this fresh, clean world. The limbs make music, too, as the breeze blows freely

QUANTICO CREEK, VIRGINIA:
left–winter along Quantico Creek;
top–winter in Prince William Forest Park;
right–mushrooms

through the pines or scrapes two oaks together. All is accompanied by the clicking voices of juncos, and we may follow the flights of cardinals and the prowlings of quail coveys.

One January day in an icy swamp we found that the first spring flowers had started to bloom. Skunk cabbage leaves had just unfurled to reveal the flowering heads inside, attracting the insects that might emerge in sunny moments.

When spring becomes more firmly entrenched, the signs of it are seen among curling hollows of leaves where bloodroot seedlings come up out of the ground. In sheltered swales along the creek are certain flats that sunlight warms enough to bring out whole displays of yellow lilies.

By this time the vireo and the cardinal sing with gusto and the wren's song fills the woods. There are now so many sounds that it takes an experienced ear to tell them apart, especially those of warblers that are passing through the trees on spring migration.

The flora fills the air with scents almost forgotten through the winter, and presents the hiker with sights of delight and joy. One day we found a tulip tree flower on the ground, unusual because the blossoms are mostly borne too high to be seen and are so sturdily attached that they seldom fall. Surprised by such a rare gift we took it over to a shaft of light where the sun picked out the brilliant yellow and orange of the petals and made them shine like polished gold.

When summer is introduced by the mountain laurel, a walk along Quantico Creek, under head-high bowers of pink and white, is a splendid way of shedding urban woes—or at least of putting them into perspective. The leaves of all the trees come out in full, and the forest shadows deepen. Crawfish build their chimneys on the muddy banks. Birds let their presence be known by a flourish of music and a flash of color.

Along Quantico Creek high water "combs" the streamside grasses and lays them neatly over rocks in a downstream direction. Rafts of bubbles and leaves float across the pools, and through the clear waters may be seen the rocks of the riverbed: quartz in white, yellow, orange, and brown; schist and slabs of grayish slate; granite in chunks of black and white that glitter with mica.

Blue damselflies perch on pebbles at the surface, and minnows scurry away in the shallows. Spiders with fascinating shapes weave webs among the leaves.

The summer forest is often full of mushrooms: shaggy-stemmed, umbrella-like, puffed, flat, and shaped like coral, goblets, cups, or saucers. They grow on logs or come up through the layer of leaves, perhaps even lifting the leaves on top of their heads, and occur in a rainbow of colors: red, yellow, purple, orange, brown, gold, gray, green, black, white, splotched, and speckled.

Late in summer the hickory nuts start falling and soon are strewn across the forest floor. The pervasive, high-pitched whine of insects adds to the singing of the stream, the calls of birds, and the twanging of frogs. Termites have been at work on an old cherry tree that died years ago. A tulip tree leaf hangs impaled on a limb, put there perhaps by a recent storm.

Chickadee chatter fills the trees. A spider hangs its net in a catbrier thicket and suspends an egg sac on a silken cable, while a slender walkingstick explores the outside of the web.

With a little more persistence it is entirely possible to observe the white-tailed deer living wild in this suburban sanctuary. There are numerous habitats besides those of the stream, and one can hike through meadows, fields, upland deciduous forests, and groves of pine. Among the sights that await the patient observer are fox, turkey, grouse, raccoon, opossum, woodchuck, squirrel, and a host of other species.

Autumn is a time of splendid, dry, sharp days when the woods and the forest floor ignite with color: The leaves of tulip trees take on a brilliant yellow; those of hickories change to gold; sassafras turns to bronze, beeches to brown, black gums to scarlet, and sweetgums to purple. Even the poison ivy presents a handsome show of red and green.

The birds sing less at this time of year, and the forest becomes more quiet. Quantico Creek runs lower in volume, but its pools remain, and on them fall the autumn leaves, which drift on the darkened waters like golden stars in space.

*　　*　　*

A secret place so close to the city allows repeated visits—to follow the course of the seasons, to feel the wind and rain, to get out at night for new adventures, to picnic, photograph, study.

It is not necessary to have a nearby Glacier Bay in order to escape the rigors of urban life and become engulfed in some of the unforgettable beauties and experiences of nature.

One does not have to explore a lava tube in California to find himself exhilarated.

To take off a day and do "absolutely nothing," to become immensely refreshed as we did at Montezuma Well, is perfectly possible almost anywhere; finding the place is rarely, if ever, as difficult as finding the time and convincing oneself that it ought to be done. The point of leisure, of course, is not to do nothing, but to do something different.

We need not wait for icebergs or arches or deserts or twisted juniper trees if we want to see intriguing forms. The bark of a birch is an example of the natural sculpture and design that surround us.

It is not essential to have the sound of the desert sparrow or the chuck-will's-widow or the *coqui* or the kittiwake before we can appreciate nature's music. A wren will do.

And there seems no valid reason for postponing a walk in the woods until we can arrive at some exotic forest of Sitka spruce, or cottonwood, or tabonuco. The woods of home can give us quite the same effect if we let them, day or night, rain or shine, summer or winter.

Prince William Forest Park has more than 35 miles of trails, but we can hardly do more than 5 of them in a single day. We are too often getting sidetracked. Along the stream we can swim if we find a pool that is big enough, and since the creek and its branches lie within the park, there is not much trouble from pollution.

A person can fuss all day over making photographs if he wants the right effect on Indian pipes or pipsissewa or a leaf with the sun shining through it.

He can assemble collections of tape recordings and build a library of wildlife sounds. He can determine what crafts are made from renewable natural resources or what wild foods are good to eat and then get practice in the lore of the woods (as long as he abides by park regulations).

He can paint or sketch, observe the clouds, identify ferns and insects or whatever he happens to see, hunt for the hiding places of moles and shrews and reptiles, seek out the nests of resident birds, observe the behavior of different species (ethology is an infant science), and try to find out what the insects have to do with the birds and the birds with the mammals and the mammals with the vegetation—the circular cyclic flow of energy in the natural world.

If the visit must be extended, there are campgrounds and picnic areas available for public use.

And if in the end the weary hiker comes back home exhausted, it is only because he has given his maximum energy to a different way of life. For a few hours he separated from himself and joined another world. But in his exhaustion he feels a special lift that does not come to him on afternoons spent wondering what to do, or watching someone else do something different. The universe was his to command, and for a while he commanded it.

Secret places such as Prince William Forest Park are easily accessible. Most American homes are within a day's drive of some long-distance footpath such as the Appalachian Trail or the Pacific Crest Trail, and there are thousands of state and municipal sanctuaries. Information about all of these is available from offices in state and national capitals.

If a man is exasperated that there are no wooded tracts within easy reach he can go to work with his congressman, councilman, or other public official to get one or more established. He can contact local societies of conservation, join the Nature Conservancy to channel his talents and riches, or simply produce in his own back yard the finest garden in the county.

The Garden Club of Plainfield, New Jersey, bought a blighted lot downtown, prepared a planting, landscaping, and color plan, and in due time built what the ladies called a "vest pocket park." They planted holly, yew, and flowering crab, set up benches, and established a maintenance crew of club volunteers. Vandalism and litter proved to be no problem. "People do not have to enter the park to enjoy it," a club member said proudly. "Walking or driving by offers a glimpse of peaceful symmetry."

A community is saved not so much by the righteous men within it, said Henry David Thoreau, but by the woods and swamps around it.

When trying out a new secret place, we attempt to get some data about it and read and study as much as possible in advance, because time may be too precious to allow much reading while visiting the site. For example, Appa-lachian Trail clubs publish a number of detailed guides so that a hiker can fol-low the route with ease and not miss important things to see along the way. Most state and local parks have maps that show the roads and trails as well as unexpected points of interest.

Local librarians can ferret out a great deal of information. The current edition of *Books in Print* should list the latest published material. County, state, or federal agencies possess a wealth of accumulated data. We try to contact state historical societies in the capital cities en route or representatives in loca-tions closer to the site. They have always given us a warm reception, and indeed seem enthusiastic about having people become involved.

The hardest part is allowing sufficient time. If the time available has to be limited, we cull some of the things we want to do and leave them for a later trip. This saves a little time for unforeseen side trips (the kind that come up where we least expect them) or for just loafing and thinking. We have never had to worry about what to do with "leftover" time.

If we let it, the sun seems to surge into our souls and brighten our spir-its. The presence of living things, of primeval rock and earth, of wind and the elements, makes us feel once more that we belong to the earth and are not set apart from it.

And that is a happy belonging. It is also a living reply to the lady who asked, "Whatever do you do out here, all by yourself?"

For Further Reading

GLACIER BAY, ALASKA

Bohn, Dave. *Glacier Bay: The Land and the Silence.* San Francisco: Sierra Club Books, 1967.

Daly, Reginald Aldworth. *The Changing World of the Ice Age.* New York: Hafner Publishing Co., 1963.

Muir, John. *Travels in Alaska.* Boston: Houghton Mifflin Co., 1915.

Wolfe, Linnie Marsh. *Son of the Wilderness: The Life of John Muir.* New York: Alfred A. Knopf, 1945.

LAVA BEDS, CALIFORNIA

Bullard, Fred M. *Volcanoes: In History, in Theory, in Eruption.* Austin: University of Texas Press, 1962.

Murray, Keith A. *The Modocs and Their War.* Norman: University of Oklahoma Press, 1959.

PLACE OF REFUGE, HAWAII

Clemens, Samuel (Mark Twain). *Roughing It.* New York: Airmont Publishing Co., Inc., 1967.

Ellis, William. *A Narrative of a Tour Through Hawaii.* Honolulu: Hawaiian Gazette Co., Ltd., 1917.

ARCHES, UTAH

Abbey, Edward. *Desert Solitaire: A Season in the Wilderness.* New York: McGraw-Hill Book Co., 1968.

Crampton, C. Gregory. *Standing Up Country: The Canyon Lands of Utah and Arizona.* New York: Alfred A. Knopf, 1964.

Harrison, Bertrand F., et al. *Plants of Arches National Monument.* Provo, Utah: Brigham Young University Press, 1964.

PRAIRIE DU CHIEN, WISCONSIN

Beaumont, William. *Experiments and Observations on the Gastric Juice and the Physiology of Digestion.* New York: Dover Publications, Inc., 1959.

Butterfield, C. W. *History of Crawford and Richland Counties, Wisconsin.* Springfield, Illinois: Union Publishing Co., 1884.

Chittenden, Hiram Martin. *The American Fur Trade of the Far West.* New York: Francis P. Harper, 1902.

Coues, Elliott, ed. *Expeditions of Zebulon Montgomery Pike to Head-Waters of the Mississippi River During the Years 1805–6–7.* New York: Francis P. Harper, 1895.

Mahan, Bruce E. *Old Fort Crawford and the Frontier.* Iowa City: State Historical Society of Iowa, 1926.

Myer, Jesse S. *Life and Letters of Dr. William Beaumont.* St. Louis: C.V. Mosby Co., 1912.

Ritzenthaler, Robert. *The Effigy Mound Builders in Wisconsin.* Milwaukee: Milwaukee Public Museum, 1969.

Rowe, Chandler W. *The Effigy Mound Culture of Wisconsin.* Milwaukee: Milwaukee Public Museum, 1956.

Scanlan, Peter L. *Prairie du Chien: French, British, American.* Menasha, Wisconsin: Banta Publishing Co., 1937.

Shetrone, Henry Clyde. *The Mound Builders.* Port Washington, New York: Kennikat Press, Inc., 1964.

Steck, Francis Borgia. *The Jolliet-Marquette Expedition.* Washington, D.C.: Catholic University of America Press, 1927.

206

NATCHEZ TRACE
TENNESSEE-ALABAMA-MISSISSIPPI

Abernethy, Thomas Perkins. *The Burr Conspiracy.* Magnolia, Massachusetts: Peter Smith, 1968.

Coates, Robert M. *The Outlaw Years: The History of the Land Pirates of the Natchez Trace.* Ann Arbor, Michigan: Midway Press, 1969.

Daniels, Jonathan. *The Devil's Backbone: The Story of the Natchez Trace.* New York: McGraw-Hill Book Co., 1962.

Dillon, Richard. *Meriwether Lewis, A Biography.* New York: Coward-McCann, Inc., 1965.

Holmes, Jack D. L. *Gayoso: The Life of a Spanish Governor in the Mississippi Valley 1789–1799.* Baton Rouge: Louisiana State University Press, 1965.

James, D. Clayton. *Antebellum Natchez.* Baton Rouge: Louisiana State University Press, 1968.

Kane, Harnett T. *Natchez on the Mississippi.* New York: William Morrow & Co., Inc., 1947.

Phelps, Dawson A. *The Natchez Trace: Indian Trail to Parkway.* Tupelo, Mississippi: Natchez Trace Parkway, n.d.

Snydor, Charles S. *A Gentleman of the Old Natchez Region.* Durham, North Carolina: Duke University Press, 1938.

EL YUNQUE, PUERTO RICO

Bond, James. *Birds of the West Indies.* Boston: Houghton Mifflin Co., 1961.

Little, Elbert L., and Wadsworth, Frank H. *Common Trees of Puerto Rico and the Virgin Islands* (U.S. Department of Agriculture Handbook No. 249). Washington, D.C.: Government Printing Office, 1964.

CARRY PONDS, MAINE

Codman, John. *Arnold's Expedition to Quebec.* New York: The Macmillan Co., 1901.

Coffin, Robert B. Tristram. *Kennebec, Cradle of Americans.* New York: Farrar & Rinehart, 1937.

Roberts, Kenneth. *Arundel.* New York: Doubleday & Co., Inc., 1956.

———, ed. *March to Quebec: Journals of the Members of Arnold's Expedition.* New York: Doubleday, Doran & Co., Inc., 1938.

Van Doren, Carl. *Secret History of the American Revolution.* New York: Viking Press, 1941.

ABOUT THE AUTHORS

ANN and MYRON SUTTON traveled 50,000 miles in the preparation of text and photographs for this book.

Ann is a geologist and Myron a botanist. With their sons, Michael, 14, and Larry, 11, they have traveled in most of the United States and to parts of Canada, Mexico, the Caribbean, Central and South America, Europe, and Asia in connection with their writing and photography.

Ann, a native of Illinois, has taught at the University of Kentucky and served with the United States Geological Survey. Myron, an Arizonan and a graduate of Northern Arizona University, is with the National Park Service, United States Department of the Interior. The Suttons have written 14 books, including *The Appalachian Trail* and *The American West: A Natural History*. Their latest juvenile book is *New Worlds for Wildlife*.